By Ronald M. Fisher
Photographed by Dick Durrance II
Foreword by Benton MacKaye

Prepared by the Special Publications Division,
National Geographic Society,
Washington, D.C.

The Appalachian Trail

THE APPALACHIAN TRAIL

By RONALD M. FISHER
National Geographic Staff
Photographed by DICK DURRANCE II
National Geographic Photographer

Published by
THE NATIONAL GEOGRAPHIC SOCIETY
MELVIN M. PAYNE, *President*
MELVILLE BELL GROSVENOR, *Editor-in-Chief*
GILBERT M. GROSVENOR, *Editor*
ANDREW H. BROWN, *Consulting Editor*

Prepared by
THE SPECIAL PUBLICATIONS DIVISION
ROBERT L. BREEDEN, *Editor*
DONALD J. CRUMP, *Associate Editor*
PHILIP B. SILCOTT, *Senior Assistant Editor*
MERRILL WINDSOR, *Manuscript Editor*
MARGERY G. DUNN, *Research and Style*
MARGARET L. DUGDALE, *Research*

Illustrations
BRYAN HODGSON, *Picture Editor*
MARGERY G. DUNN, WILLIAM R. GRAY,
    H. ROBERT MORRISON, *Picture Legends*
JILL DURRANCE, *Picture Legend Research*

Layout and Design
JOSEPH A. TANEY, *Staff Art Director*
JOSEPHINE B. BOLT, *Art Director*
URSULA PERRIN, *Design Assistant*
PAUL M. BREEDEN, *Calligraphy*
PAUL SALMON, *Map Design*
JOHN D. GARST, JR., VIRGINIA L. BAZA, MONICA
    WOODBRIDGE, *Map Research*
TIBOR TOTH, *Map Relief*
ISKANDAR BADAY, BETTY CLONINGER, ELIE SABBAN,
    ALFRED ZEBARTH, LEO ZEBARTH, *Map Production*

Production and Printing
ROBERT W. MESSER, *Production Manager*
MARGARET MURIN SKEKEL, RAJA D. MURSHED,
    Production Assistants
JAMES R. WHITNEY, JOHN R. METCALFE, *Engraving
    and Printing*
MARTA I. BERNAL, SUZANNE J. JACOBSON, ELIZABETH
    VAN BEUREN JOY, JOAN PERRY, *Staff Assistants*
BARBARA KLEIN, ANNE MCCAIN, *Index*

SECOND PRINTING 1973

Standard Book Number 87044-106-X
Library of Congress Catalog Card Number 72-75380

*"The ultimate purpose of the Appala-
chian Trail?" ponders Benton MacKaye,
its 93-year-old founder. "To walk. To
see. And to see what you see." In the half
century since 1921, the dream of this
craggy naturalist from Massachusetts
has materialized into a wilderness footpath extending 2,015 miles from Maine
to Georgia.*

*Overleaf: In a serene North Carolina forest, the trail winds through
fir and spruce undergrown with ferns. Page 1: Perched on a stump in
Georgia, a catbird breaks the early-morning calm. Endpapers: Wild
turkeys make their way through a clearing near the trail in southwestern Virginia. Bookbinding: Monogram of the Appalachian Trail.*
ENDPAPER DRAWING BY GEORGE FOUNDS

*I*T MAY HAVE BEEN in 1891, while I was listening to bearded, one-armed Maj. John Wesley Powell recount to an enthralled audience in Washington City his historic trip through the Grand Canyon....

It may have been in 1897, in the White Mountains of New Hampshire, as Sturgis Pray and I struggled through a tangled blowdown....

Or it may have been in 1900 when I stood with another friend, Horace Hildreth, viewing the heights of the Green Mountains....

Somewhere, sometime back there near the end of the old century, the notion of an Appalachian Trail occurred to me. But it wasn't until 1921 that the idea had crystallized. On Sunday, July 10, at Hudson Guild Farm in New Jersey, I sat down with Charles H. Whitaker, editor of the *Journal* of the American Institute of Architects, and Clarence S. Stein, chairman of the AIA's Committee on Community Planning. I explained my idea for a trail that would run in a wilderness belt from one of the highest mountains in New England to one of the highest in the South.

Both friends encouraged me to write an article setting forth the idea. I did, and in October 1921 the *Journal* of the AIA published "An Appalachian Trail, A Project in Regional Planning."

Then came years of conferring, routing, brush-cutting, mapping, consulting with Forest and Park Services. From the beginning, the trail's existence and success were dependent on the good will of countless individuals — notably volunteer workers and cooperative landowners.

Men whose names now are often forgotten contributed as much to getting the project launched as did I: newspaperman Raymond Torrey, forester Verne Rhoades, geologist François Matthes, Dr. H. S. Hedges, and Maj. W. A. Welch, who presided at the first meeting of the Appalachian Trail Conference in 1925.

The creation of the ATC was one of two pivotal events in the history of the trail; the other was the signing of the National Trails System Act in 1968. The first provided a parent organization for clubs whose members work at maintaining the trail; the second provided federal protection for it. Achieving this protected status is the result of the enthusiasm and concern of a host of hikers during half a century. Perhaps it is unrivaled by any other single feat in the development of American outdoor recreation.

I find in this a note of optimism for our sometimes gloomy world. With pollution and overpopulation spawning a sprawling urban desert, I am encouraged by the knowledge that there are millions in America who care about wilderness and mountains; who go for strength to Mother Earth; who defend her domain and seek her secrets.

I am proud to have played a role in the birth of the Appalachian Trail. And I am proud of the generations of hikers who have made my dream become a reality.

BENTON MACKAYE

Evening sun frames a white oak bud just opening in May atop 4,461-foot Blood Mountain,

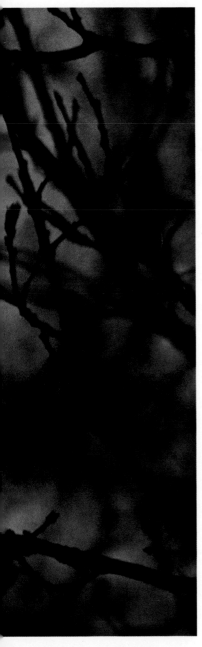

the trail's crest in Georgia.

A long, thin strip of America

THE FIRST THING that struck me about the Appalachian Trail was that it all seemed uphill. It's not, of course. For every mountain you climb, there's a valley beyond.

My second reaction was an appreciation of its length. For most hikers —excepting those few hardy souls who tackle the whole thing—the trail has no end. It winds for 2,015 miles through the great Appalachian mountain system of the Atlantic states, from Springer Mountain in northern Georgia to Mount Katahdin in central Maine. You could take hiking vacations on it for years and never cover the same ground twice.

My third—and most lasting—response was one of gratitude: that the trail *exists*, that it has survived megalopolis, a motorized population, and ready-mixed concrete. The Appalachian Trail is a splendid and precious thing, a lonely, extended retreat brushing against the country's most populous region. More than 125 million Americans live within a day's drive of it!

When I arrived in Atlanta early in May 1971 to meet NATIONAL GEOGRAPHIC photographer Dick Durrance and his wife Jill, I was an authentic rookie as far as hiking was concerned. I'd done some camping and had gone on a few fishing trips, but hiking and the Appalachian Trail were both new to me. Our plan was to start at Springer Mountain and follow the trail north, picking interesting portions to hike, but spending much of our time exploring the surrounding countryside and meeting the people who live there.

We were not disappointed. On our way to Katahdin we encountered moonshiners, Indians, and bird-watchers in the south; dairy farmers, ranger-naturalists, and craftsmen in the central section; marble quarrymen, rock climbers, and loggers in the north.

Bronze plaque atop Springer Mountain in Georgia marks the southern end of the Appalachian Trail. Here author Ron Fisher, with photographer Dick Durrance and his wife Jill, started on a six-month hiking adventure.

We visited 14 states, eight national forests, two national parks, and several state preserves. We wound through rhododendron thickets and crossed bald, windswept mountaintops in Tennessee. We climbed peaks of the Blue Ridge in southwestern Virginia and crisscrossed Skyline Drive in the Shenandoah National Park. We looked down on the dramatic setting of Harpers Ferry, West Virginia, where the Shenandoah River rushes into the Potomac; we communed with the ghosts of a vanished coal and iron community in Pennsylvania. In New Hampshire we climbed above timberline in the Presidential Range, and in Maine we plunged into a wet wilderness of spruce and birch, lakes and ponds — "Maine is at least 90 percent water," another hiker had warned me.

In six months we sampled a long, thin strip of America.

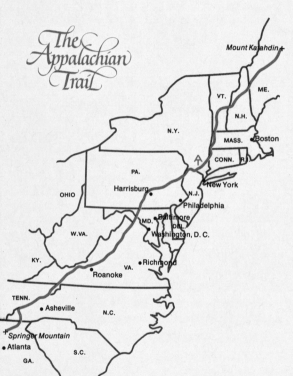

Georgia was at its greenest as we drove north by jeep from Atlanta. Spring had come with a joyous splash; the roadsides above red clay banks were dazzling with the fresh green of new leaves and the bright pink of azalea blossoms.

We pitched our tents at the foot of Springer Mountain in Amicalola Falls State Park, established in 1948 to protect the silvery, 500-foot cascades whose lilting name is the Cherokee word for "tumbling waters."

The campground proved typical of those the tourists demand nowadays: electricity at every site, concrete picnic tables, a bathhouse with hot showers and washer and drier. After a supper of reconstituted chicken Romanoff, I unrolled my sleeping bag under a full moon and scudding clouds.

But the campground wasn't ready for bed yet. Tent zippers rasped, and butane lanterns shone like spotlights no matter which way I turned. Irritable infants chorused a not-very-comforting lullaby. Late-comers used their headlights to search for campsites, raced engines, slammed car doors; children laughed, mothers called, and harassed fathers shouted.

Then it began to rain—at first a gentle sprinkle, but enough to move me into my tent. Thunder rumbled across the mountains; a bolt of lightning illumined the inside of the tent like a flashbulb; a deafening thunderclap burst the heavens, and suddenly all the water in the firmament poured down. The rain's tattoo on my plastic roof sounded like the frenzied action in a popcorn popper.

The heaviest downpour was soon over, but for a while I lay listening to the rain and thinking about the footpath we would start walking next day.

Contrary to the impression of many Americans that it is an old pioneer track, the Appalachian Trail was born only half a century ago, the brain-child of a remarkable gentleman named Benton MacKaye. A native of Stamford, Connecticut, he grew up in New York City and Shirley Center, Massachusetts. His father was an entrepreneur who produced, among other things, Buffalo Bill's Wild West show.

Now 93, Mr. MacKaye lives with a niece in Shirley Center. In the foreword to this book he recounts how he conceived the idea of a hiking trail that would reach the length of the Appalachians, how friends helped him rally support, and how the plan caught on.

The first portion actually cleared and marked was finished in 1923 in the Bear Mountain section of the Palisades Interstate Park of New York and New Jersey. In 1925 the Appalachian Trail Conference was established in Washington, D. C., to coordinate work on the project, and by the time of its second meeting in 1928 a total of some 500 miles of trail was ready for hikers. By 1931 nearly two-thirds of the planned route was done, and six years later—in August 1937—the trail was completed.

As interest increased over the years, so did the number of hiking clubs in areas along the route. Affiliated through the Appalachian Trail Conference, these clubs did most of the work of clearing the trail. Today some 100,000 hikers belong to more than a hundred ATC-associated groups.

During World War II few people had time for recreational hiking—and many a soldier was sure he would never want to hike again. The neglected trail deteriorated. But with the war's end, outdoors enthusiasts pitched in and the entire route was restored in surprisingly short order.

By 1958 chicken farms had begun to crowd Mount Oglethorpe, so the southern terminus was shifted to Springer Mountain, 13 miles north. But the problem was more general than that; concrete and steel threatened other parts of the trail. Sections crossing privately owned land were also vulnerable in another way: Some owners had legitimate complaints that had changed their attitude toward the trail. With the ever-growing numbers of hikers came rowdy crowds and thoughtless individuals who scattered litter, left gates open, and sometimes destroyed property.

Clearly some kind of protected status was needed. On October 2, 1968, President Lyndon B. Johnson signed into law the National Trails System Act, establishing two federally protected trails—the Appalachian and the 2,400-mile Pacific Crest—and providing a basis for developing others.

A T SOME POINT I fell asleep, and then suddenly it was morning. More rain seemed likely when we emerged from our sleeping bags and peered at the overcast sky. We folded the tents, ate breakfast, laced our boots, filled canteens, and piled back into the jeep for the short trip to Nimblewill Gap and the approach trail that would take us 2.3 miles to the summit of Springer Mountain.

A series of guidebooks—ten in all—available from the Appalachian Trail Conference gives detailed instructions for reaching and following the trail. The paragraph on the approach section we were about to tackle reads: "Cross road in Nimblewill Gap and continue at first steeply, then more gradually up flat ridge to summit of Black Mtn. (3,600 ft.) at 5.4 m. . . . Continue over Black Mtn. and descend into gap (3,400 ft.) at 5.7 m. Follow flat ridge to level section with scrub pine at 6.2 m., then zigzag steeply up slope. Reach the Appalachian Trail at its southern terminus on the summit of Springer Mtn. (3,782 ft.) at 6.9 m."

The very first "steeply" left me in a panting heap beside the trail. My mouth was full of cotton, my calves were aching, my heart—unaccustomed to such demands—was surely going to burst. Dick and Jill, conditioned athletes, disappeared up the slope, chatting casually.

I caught up with them finally on Black Mountain, where they mercifully lifted my thousand-pound pack from my back. Revived by a drink of warm lemonade, I eventually made it to the top of Springer. Two indigo buntings accompanied me part way, chirping encouragement, the flash of their brilliant plumage always one shrub ahead of me. On the summit we found a plaque embedded in a boulder, dated 1934 and showing a hiker striding northward.

After supper we sprawled on a rocky ledge to watch the sun dip behind the Blue Ridge. As dusk fell, I pondered the peculiar nature of hikers: perverse souls who endure rain and cold, blisters and austere rations, uncomfortable beds and unfriendly bugs, not to mention the simple hard labor of carrying a heavy pack uphill. For what? A glimpse of a bird? A breath of clean air? A sunset? A mountain panorama, flowers and trees, a few hours of solitude?

They're an enigmatic group, I would find. I remembered the story of a backpacker who emerged from the trail into the parking lot at Newfound Gap in the Tennessee-North Carolina Smokies. A pudgy, sandaled tourist hailed him: "Hey, buddy, where's that path lead to?"

The hiker silenced him with one word: "Maine."

And that's where we were headed.

Backpackers amble through blueberry thickets ablaze with autumn near the summit of Rainbow Ledges in Maine, a 20-mile hike from Katahdin— "greatest mountain" to Penobscot Indians—the trail's northernmost point.

"Man came up
once from Atlanta
and wanted to buy
some onions.
'No, you can't buy
none,' I said, 'but
I'll give you some.'"

Weathered skin of Georgia farmer James M. Gravitt, 77, matches the earth he hoes. "I been doing this all my life," he said, turning the soil of his garden near Gainesville for spring planting of peas, lima beans, corn, and onions. Spring also brings the colorful flowering of wild native plants. A redbud tree's blossoms open directly from the branch; flame azalea (left) ranges from orange to scarlet; orange stamens tip a delicate foamflower.

Lone horse prances among cattle heading home at sundown in Wear Cove, Tennessee, a meadowed valley in the Great Smoky Mountains. The trail skirts many such coves in this secluded back country where hardy folk live and work the land. "The longer we were out on the trail," said Dick, "the more we gained a sense of the land, the people, and nature. We began to understand our relationship to the environment, to appreciate how fragile and priceless it is—and it became very important to us."

N.G.S. PHOTOGRAPHER BRUCE DALE

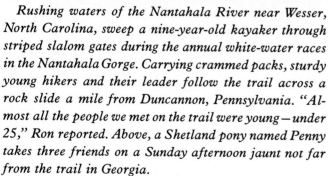

Rushing waters of the Nantahala River near Wesser, North Carolina, sweep a nine-year-old kayaker through striped slalom gates during the annual white-water races in the Nantahala Gorge. Carrying crammed packs, sturdy young hikers and their leader follow the trail across a rock slide a mile from Duncannon, Pennsylvania. "Almost all the people we met on the trail were young—under 25," Ron reported. Above, a Shetland pony named Penny takes three friends on a Sunday afternoon jaunt not far from the trail in Georgia.

Spiders' webs cling to tall stems of spent Queen Anne's lace in a field beside the High Meadows Sugar House, near Bromley Mountain in Vermont. In early spring, sugarers will tap maple trees, draw the sap into buckets, and carry it to this little house where wood fires boil it into sweet maple syrup. It takes 40 gallons of sap to make just one gallon of syrup. "It's a tricky business," a veteran sugarer explained. "To get the right pressure to make the sap run, we need a stretch of spring weather that alternates freezing nights with warm days."

After breaking camp at sunrise and hiking for a couple of hours in a leafy Maine forest, Ron and Jill cook a breakfast of freeze-dried eggs, hashed brown potatoes, and cocoa. "Meals were among the highlights of each day," said Jill. Hoping for a handout, a chipmunk waits alertly on a branch; a ruffed grouse peers from a red spruce.

"Again today two chipmunks joined us for breakfast."

Poor of sight, a banded argiope spider with an inch-long body waits for vibrations to signal that its prey is in the web. Raindrops dapple the back of a red maple leaf on a bed of lichens. Icicles hang from a snowy rock above a brook. "At first we only saw the big things—mountains, the skyline," said Jill. "But the more we walked, the more selective our vision became, and we began to notice the beauty of mosses and berries and drops of water; we'd get on our hands and knees for a closer look."

Gliding on new snow, members of the Dartmouth Outing Club ski along the trail at the foot of Smarts Mountain in New Hampshire. Near Hanover, skiers collect sap-filled buckets from maple trees. "We were amazed at the way so many people use the trail for such different purposes," Ron observed. "Hiking, ski touring, rock climbing, or just watching birds, flowers, and animals—every season has its pastime, and every pastime has its enthusiasts."

1.

From Chattahoochee to Nantahala

WE AWOKE in a cloud: Thick, cottony mist had settled over our mountaintop during the night. Inside my tent the moisture condensed on the sloping surface and dripped onto my sleeping bag; outside, heavy dew glistened on grass and ferns, and within 20 yards the trail vanished in the fog. But by the time we had eaten and packed up, the morning was clearing rapidly, and we set off down Springer Mountain in bright sunshine.

For its first 78 miles, until it reaches the North Carolina border, the trail lies within the Chattahoochee National Forest. *Chattahoochee* is Cherokee for "flower painted rock," and throughout this region waterfalls and wild flowers brighten the rocky slopes.

It was hot on the trail and very quiet, except for the distant hammering of a woodpecker and the soft creaking of two dead tree limbs rubbing together in the wind. For several hours the only wildlife we sighted was a squirrel that darted across the trail just ahead of us. We hiked through arches of creamy-flowered rhododendrons, drank from a clear spring, and cooled our feet in the waters of Chester Creek.

At Stover Creek we stopped for lunch, and decided to make a game of identifying trees. But of the 125 kinds or more that grow in the Chattahoochee, we saw only a few that day—mostly bold-leafed maples, finer-foliaged ashes and elms, white pines, short-needled hemlocks, and handsome tulip trees still showing a few lingering greenish-yellow blossoms.

The only person we met was a woman from Cincinnati who was back-tracking in search of her Labrador retriever, Thor. Since the dog's disappearance several days before, she and her husband—now off checking

De Soto Falls drops 600 feet in less than a third of a mile in the Chattahoochee National Forest, Georgia. Spanish soldiers led by Hernando de Soto explored this wilderness in 1540.

"The first thing that struck me about the Appalachian Trail was that it all seemed uphill."

a side trail—had been retracing their steps, calling Thor's name and putting out food. We talked awhile, and wished her luck.

Near the summit of Hawk Mountain we came to an abandoned fire tower. Just over the crest lay a meadow of ankle-high grass, framed by forest. We found a spring and a wooden lean-to, and here we camped.

Altogether 226 lean-to shelters have been built along the trail over the years. Some were put up by the Civilian Conservation Corps during the 1930's; others have been added by the Forest Service, national and state park services, and hiking clubs. Often it is necessary to share them with mice, but that is a minor matter when cold or rain threatens. Some of the shelters have built-in wooden or wire bunks, and all are inscribed with the accumulated graffiti of the years. The most prominent message in ours declared, "I was miserable here." But we pulled off our boots with sighs of great satisfaction, and Dick quickly had a fire crackling.

I scoffed when Jill checked the guidebook and said we had covered only a little more than nine miles that day; I was sure we had come five times that far. In minutes I was asleep, forgetting both my sunburned neck and the mice.

Early next morning we began the long descent into Hightower Gap. Occasionally a U. S. Army helicopter passed over at low altitude, reminding us of a guidebook warning: "It is frightening, but not dangerous, to come upon camouflaged soldiers under simulated combat conditions. . . ." I had the unsettling sensation all morning that I was being watched, but we saw no one. Later we learned more about the Army's Ranger training in military mountaineering and patrolling when we talked to Lt. Col. Everett Yon at the Mountain Ranger Camp on the Dahlonega-Cooper Gap road.

"Rangers spend 18 days here with us," he explained. "They also train at Fort Benning and in the Florida swamps, and we're trying to add a fourth phase in the desert at Fort Bliss, Texas. Here, we teach them how to turn conditions of mountainous terrain to their advantage."

Colonel Yon introduced us to Capt. John H. Armstrong, a tall young instructor who invited us to accompany some of his men on a training

exercise. In his jeep we bounced down dusty back roads to a rendezvous with a squad of combat veterans from Fort Benning who would play the role of the enemy. The plan was to move along a section of trail where Rangers were waiting to ambush us—if we didn't spot them first.

Quietly, single file, we set out. M-14 rifles cradled in their arms, our companions moved as stealthily as wary animals, and I wondered what memories of other, distant trails this exercise evoked.

I started violently at a rifle shot up ahead; then came another, followed by rapid firing and the burst of a machine gun. Shouting men dashed past us; a red smoke grenade sent sparrows winging off in fright.

Within a couple of minutes all was quiet again. Our patrol had discovered the Rangers' position before they could launch the ambush.

As we started back up the trail with Captain Armstrong, we asked whether hikers interfered with the training.

"We don't see very many," he said, "and they don't bother us. As a matter of fact, sometimes we can help them—show them where to find water, where to camp, maybe give them a ride."

Spent blank cartridges littered the trail, but Armstrong indicated they wouldn't be there long. "Local people come pick up the brass; I think they can get about 22 cents a pound for it. They might get two or three pounds from an exercise like today's."

Our goal for the night was the shelter at Gooch Gap, and there we found no shortage of wildlife. In the cold pool of a spring a salamander skittered back and forth; shortly after dark an owl began to hoot, and repeated its soft, hollow notes until abruptly silenced by the scream of a bobcat that seemed only yards from our campfire.

In the morning we walked the three and a half miles to the trail-road intersection at Woody Gap, where a friend had left our car.

The gap is named for a memorable Georgian, Arthur Woody, who served for 30 years as chief ranger of the 250,000-acre Blue Ridge District of the Chattahoochee National Forest. He ruled his domain like a benevolent patriarch, acquiring more land for the preserve, patrolling—often barefooted—its trails and crests, discouraging poachers from molesting his beloved deer, refereeing feuds among the short-tempered mountaineers.

"We've had 'em bumped off pretty regular all over this country," he told a magazine interviewer in 1944, two years before his death. "Up 'til a few years back people never thought 'bout a killin' scrape as somethin' 'specially unusual."

Arguments often had violent solutions. He recalled an episode involving a man named Jep Hale, "a feller that'd strike like a rattler if anybody got in his way." Jep and his brother were waiting when three men came looking for them one night. "Had a regular battle. Rifle shots from out that window killed two of the men in the road an' tore up the other. They say it was a quarrel over likker blockadin' " — as moonshining is called in parts of the southern Appalachians.

On a hunt when he was still a boy, Woody saw his father shoot what they later decided must have been the last native white-tailed deer in Georgia. As he grew older he decided it was his responsibility to make amends, so in 1927 he obtained five fawns from another state, bottle-fed them, and kept them at his home until they were old enough to release in the forest. He repeated this until the herd was re-established, and today thousands of whitetails roam the Chattahoochee.

READY for a hot bath and soft bed, we made the short drive into Dahlonega. This somnolent village, we learned, had once been the center of a gold boom, triggered apparently by a deer hunter named Benjamin Parks in 1828. Sixty-six years later, in 1894, Mr. Parks retold his story to a reporter for the *Atlanta Constitution*. "I kicked up something that caught my eye," he said. "I examined it, and decided that it was gold. The place belonged to Rev. Mr. Obarr who, though a preacher, was a hard man. . . ."

He leased the land from Mr. Obarr, but when the hint of gold turned into a confirmed strike, the preacher demanded his lease back. Parks refused. "Two weeks later," Parks continued, "I saw a party of two men and two women approaching. I knew it was Obarr's family, intent upon trouble. Knowing Obarr's fondness for litigation, I warned my men to hold their own, but to take no offensive step.

" 'Mr. Parks,' were Obarr's first words, 'I want the mine.'

" 'If you were to pay me ten times its value,' I replied, 'I would not sell it to you.'

" 'Well, the longest pole will knock off the persimmon,' he said, threateningly. At that moment, Mrs. Obarr broke the sluice gates to let out the water. A laborer was in the ditch, and the woman threw rocks in the water, in order to splash him. Failing to make him aggressive, she burst into tears . . . her son advanced, to attack. . . . I caught him by the collar, and flung him back. . . ." Obarr then attempted to have the Parks group jailed, but without success.

Having resisted the preacher's attempt to recover the lease, Parks eventually sold it to Sen. John C. Calhoun of South Carolina for what he thought was a good price. But "the very first month after the sale, he took out 24,000 pennyweights [1,200 ounces] of gold, and then I was inclined to be mad with him, as Obarr had been with me."

Meanwhile Dahlonega was struggling to cope with the influx of prospectors. More than 10,000 placer miners were soon working the streams within a 15-mile radius of the town. For a time gold was so abundant that youngsters occasionally found nuggets worth several dollars in the streets after a rainstorm. Thirsty miners paid for their drinks with gold dust measured on the tip of a knife. Grave diggers tossed up chunks of quartz flecked with gold, causing an old-timer to comment, "The miner has the assurance that when he has laid down his pick and shovel, and panned out his last 'clean up,' his weary bones will be laid to rest within a tomb, the walls of which are glittering with the yellow metal for which he toiled his life away."

Clay for the bricks in the Dahlonega Courthouse, now a museum commemorating the gold mining days, came from Cane Creek a mile from town; every brick, it is said, contains traces of gold.

In 1838 Congress established a branch mint in Dahlonega, and in the next 23 years it coined more than $6,000,000. With the outbreak of the Civil War in 1861 the mint was closed, and for a while federal troops were quartered within its walls. The California gold rush of 1849 had lured most of Dahlonega's prospectors and small-scale miners westward. But a few mining firms continued to operate, sinking shafts into the hills around the town, until after the war.

The museum in the former courthouse preserves relics of the lively days. One of its hostesses when we visited was soft-voiced Amy Trammell, who has an authentic firsthand knowledge of Georgia's gold-mining: For 35 years she and her husband Bill, who died in 1966, panned for gold in the hills of northern Georgia. Every Monday, when the museum is closed—and if the weather is balmy—she takes her shovel and pan and disappears into the mountains.

Shyly she agreed to let Jill, Dick, and me accompany her the next Monday morning. We picked her up at her home in nearby Auraria, and she directed us to Ralston Branch, a quiet stream that runs across her property.

"Bill had a pan that had been in his family for 130 years," she said. "His grandfather came here during the boom, in 1838. Now then...."

From the stream bank she dug a shovelful of soil and dumped it into the pan. Then, immersing the pan in the flowing water, she began shaking it slightly, swirling the water, carefully washing away the lighter parts of the soil. She reminisced as she worked. "In 1958 Dahlonega donated 43 ounces of gold for the capitol in Atlanta. We all dressed up like old-timey prospectors and took it down in a wagon. Such a time! Later, after it was beaten into long strips of gold leaf, they put it on the dome."

Gradually the dirt in the pan diminished as the gentle swirling and washing continued. With the tip of her little finger, Amy brushed away the last of the mud, and there on the bottom of the pan—just a few flakes, but unmistakable—was gold!

We all took turns trying it, and under Amy's tutelage each of us scored. She brushed our findings into a tiny vial and presented the total take to Jill as a memento.

As we prepared to leave, Amy's gaze moved to the hilltops around us. "For a year after Bill died I couldn't come here," she said. "But then I thought, this is where he was happiest. Now nothing could treat me better than to get out all day panning."

From Woody Gap the trail crosses Blood, Levelland, and Cowrock Mountains, curves around the headwaters of the Chattahoochee River, climbs steeply over Tray Mountain, and dips across three gaps before it reaches the North Carolina line. It is a splendid section of the trail for hikers and campers: an area of mature, well-managed timberland that looks like a vast botanical garden when spring unfolds the bloom of rhododendrons, azaleas, and mountain laurel, and spreads a carpet of wild flowers on the forest floor.

From secluded hollows and hidden coves in this region, telltale wisps of smoke still sometimes rise, hinting at the presence of that fabled mountain character, the moonshiner. He and his adventures have been the subject of countless cartoons and jokes, but those who know most about modern moonshining see little humor in it for one convincing reason: Because of dangerous methods of illicit distilling, much moonshine whiskey is poisonous.

The Scotch-Irish immigrants who settled in the southern mountains in the 18th and early 19th centuries brought with them the techniques and traditions of home distilling. For many years their production was primarily for their own consumption, but eventually they learned a practical lesson of economics: Corn in its solid state was less profitable than in liquid form; converted to whiskey, it cost less to transport and yielded a much higher return.

In the 1920's Prohibition brought boom times to moonshiners, and in some mountain areas almost every family was involved in one way or another with production or sale of whiskey. Many neglected farming altogether to concentrate on this profitable sideline. But repeal of Prohibition in 1933 again made liquor legally available, and to stay in business moonshiners not only had to lower their prices but also to lengthen their lines of distribution. As the price went down, so did quality. More important, moonshiners increasingly used old auto and truck radiators as their condensing equipment. The soldered joints of the radiators contaminate the whiskey with poisonous — even lethal — lead salts. Federal agents annually discover thousands of stills equipped with such makeshift condensers.

As recently as 1955, University of Tennessee researchers have estimated, illicit stills produced 21 million gallons of whiskey in the southern Appalachians alone. Most of it ended up in unlicensed bars in low-income sections of large cities.

Today moonshining finally is on the decline, officials of the Internal Revenue Service believe.

"Partly it's because of better enforcement techniques," one said. "You can cover a lot of ground in a helicopter, and in the fall and winter, with the leaves off the trees, moonshiners don't have any cover. Another factor is that their former customers are getting more sophisticated about the liquor they drink. Still, we seize 3,000 to 4,000 stills a year."

Fred Goswick, who ran his first load of moonshine to Atlanta when he was 15, said to us, "The defense lawyers were the only ones to make any money from 'shine." Fred now squires tourists through his Moonshine

Museum—"the only one in the world"—in Dawsonville, Georgia. Inside a long, barnlike wooden building he has set up four stills ranging from an early copper contrivance to a model of a modern giant capable of producing 3,000 gallons of liquor a day.

"These were put together by Carl Phillips, a moonshiner from way back," he said. "He started in the business when he was 9, and he's 65 now. He's spent 69 months in jail. Federal agents come around here all the time to make sure these stills are dry."

I asked Fred why he gave up moonshining. "I had a bad car accident a few years ago, and it gave me time to think," he replied. "Now really! How can an uneducated Southern boy think he can come out ahead of the Federal Government? So I decided to open this museum. I'm not trying either to knock moonshining or to glorify it. I'm just trying to show what once was here."

BEFORE WE LEFT Georgia we paused at the Spring Country Music Festival at Hiawassee. More than a hundred musicians with fiddles, guitars, banjos, and mandolins, along with dozens of singers and dancers, performed in a tent for an enthusiastic crowd of nearly 3,000. Good humor was evident everywhere; jam sessions started up spontaneously in the parking lot, and one old-timer declared, "I'll swear, every time it gets, it gets better!"

We caught up with the Appalachian Trail again on Wayah Bald, in the Nantahala National Forest in North Carolina. A stone observation-tower memorial to John H. Byrne, former forest supervisor of the Nantahala, rises atop the mile-high mountain. From it we could see the Smokies and Mount Mitchell—6,684 feet, the Appalachians' highest—to the north, and ranges of South Carolina and Georgia in the blue haze to the south.

As the wind moaned that night over Wayah Bald, Jill insisted on reading to us from a little book of ghost stories of the southern Appalachians. One I vividly remember concerned a miner working alone at the end of a dark, deep shaft. He heard an unfamiliar, eerie hissing noise that gradually grew louder and finally swelled into an anguished, wailing tumult. The miner decided it must be the crying of all the men who had died in that mine. Abandoning his tools, he crawled and stumbled out of the shaft and made his way to the surface—and never went below ground again.

The next day's hike was leisurely, little more than five miles, to Cold Springs Trail Shelter. We met a couple on horseback—intruders on a trail that is not intended, constructed, or routed as a bridle path. Hoofs gouge holes that speed erosion and complicate maintenance.

Our pleasant campsite had not only a spring and a shelter but also a fireplace and picnic table. Buttercups and violets bloomed all around us, and a rufous-sided towhee flitted here and there in a blur of black, white, and rust red. I spread my sleeping bag beside the spring, but before the night was over we kept our record intact—at least a sprinkle of rain every night we had camped—and moved into the shelter.

Next morning we met our first fellow backpacker—a young man dressed in blue jeans, long-sleeved shirt, and high boots, sweating heavily. "Don't you ever wear shorts?" we asked him. "No," he answered, "I got bit by a snake once and that cured me. I was rock-climbing down around Springer and a copperhead bit me on the leg."

Protection against such hazards is an advantage of long, heavy trousers, and many hiking authorities recommend them, but we continued to favor the coolness and comfort of shorts—making sure we kept our snake-bite kit handy, and trying always to stay alert.

Three and a half miles beyond Cold Springs lies Tellico Gap. From there the trail crosses Wesser Bald and winds its way down to the Nantahala River. About 25 miles farther on, it reaches Fontana Dam at the southern end of Great Smoky Mountains National Park. This section is often described as the most difficult of the entire Appalachian Trail. Extremely steep ascents and descents take the hiker over ridge after ridge, through some of the most untamed country in the eastern United States.

At Wesser, North Carolina, the trail crosses the Nantahala River—and so did we, during the annual white-water races in the Nantahala Gorge. On the morning of this event the power company releases enough water from its reservoir to turn the rock-strewn river white over the entire eight-mile canoe course.

Spectators lined the bank as men, women, and children flashed by in a series of slalom events for kayaks and downriver races for canoes. The turbulent river assured plenty of spills, and the kayakers, buttoned into their unstable little craft, frequently found themselves sitting upside down in the roiling water.

But no memory of the southern Appalachians stays with me more clearly than the sound of a songbird—I still don't know what kind it was—that stayed just out of sight while offering its pure, melodic, heartlifting song. We were hiking down a mountain that afternoon, and for half a mile the elusive bird followed along. Hiding and trilling like a mad flutist, it piped us on our way.

Retired house painter Grover C. Elkins and his wife Susie relax with three of their eight dogs on their porch in Cleveland, Georgia.

"You all come back and see us."

"We raised
ten children on
nine acres of cotton,
and we raised
all the food we ate."

"Just to pass the time," Lizzie Chambers leans against a porch post in Dahlonega, Georgia; her husband Mirdy, nearly blind, sits with two of their ten children, Mary Ellen, left, and Barbara. "I'd rather live in an old chicken coop like this than in one of those mansions," said Lizzie contentedly. At far left, J. Frank Wilson stands with his wife Elva outside their home. Mr. Wilson was born in North Carolina's Nantahala Mountains in 1882 and has stayed there most of his life. He once moved to Montana for three years but grew homesick: "You could stand on top of a mountain and see a million acres. But if you gave me every bit I could see for 50 cents, I still wouldn't want it." Old wagon wheels frame James Turner's mailboxes near Blairsville, Georgia.

*Ferris wheel of Honest Homer Scott's Georgia Amusement Company whirls in Cleve-
land each May for a week of entertainment. The small carnival offers an exciting change
from routine in southern Appalachian farming communities. Ready for a portrait, Mr. and
Mrs. Otis Cleveland pose before a tropical backdrop in the photographer's stall. Two dozen
amusement stands tempt all comers to try their skill; before a row of baseball targets a
concessionaire urges everyone to "Tip Them Over" and win a doll.*

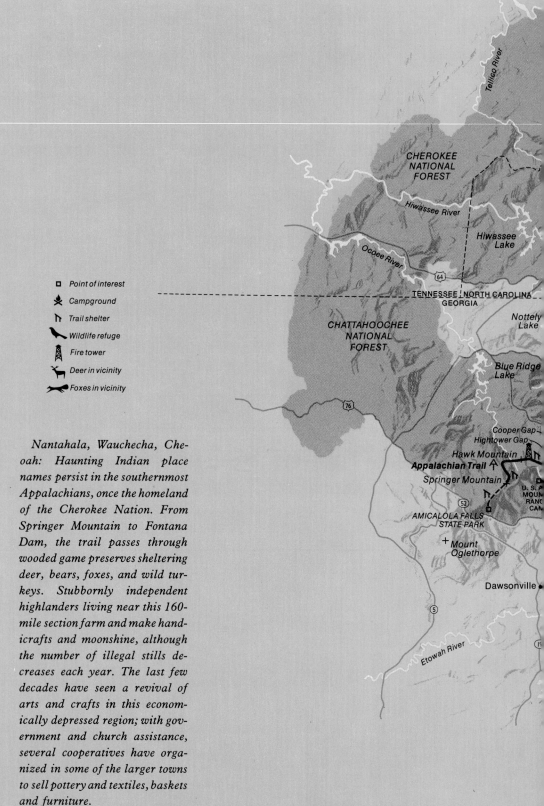

Nantahala, Wauchecha, Cheoah: Haunting Indian place names persist in the southernmost Appalachians, once the homeland of the Cherokee Nation. From Springer Mountain to Fontana Dam, the trail passes through wooded game preserves sheltering deer, bears, foxes, and wild turkeys. Stubbornly independent highlanders living near this 160-mile section farm and make handicrafts and moonshine, although the number of illegal stills decreases each year. The last few decades have seen a revival of arts and crafts in this economically depressed region; with government and church assistance, several cooperatives have organized in some of the larger towns to sell pottery and textiles, baskets and furniture.

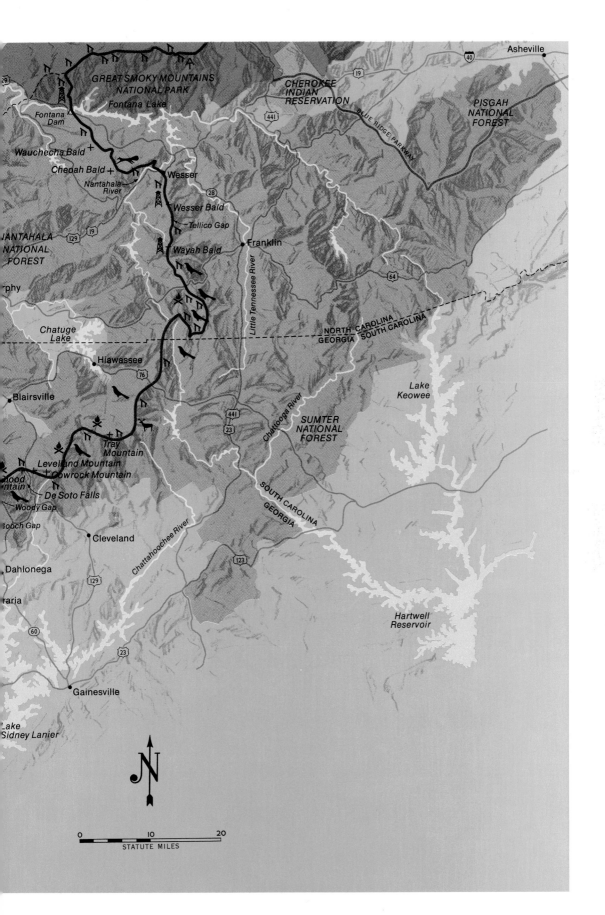

Asheville

GREAT SMOKY MOUNTAINS
NATIONAL PARK
Fontana Lake

CHEROKEE
INDIAN
RESERVATION

PISGAH
NATIONAL
FOREST

BLUE RIDGE PARKWAY

Fontana
Dam

Wauchecha Bald

Cheoah Bald

Nantahala
River

Wesser

Wesser Bald

Tellico Gap

Wayah Bald

Franklin

NANTAHALA
NATIONAL
FOREST

phy

Chatuge
Lake

NORTH CAROLINA
GEORGIA

SOUTH CAROLINA

Little Tennessee River

Lake
Keowee

Hiawassee

Blairsville

Chattooga River

SUMTER
NATIONAL
FOREST

Tray
Mountain

Levelland Mountain

Cowrock Mountain

De Soto Falls

Woody Gap

ood
ntain

SOUTH CAROLINA
GEORGIA

Gooch Gap

Cleveland

Chattahoochee River

Dahlonega

raria

Hartwell
Reservoir

Gainesville

Lake
Sidney Lanier

N

0   10   20
STATUTE MILES

43

"Enemy" machine gunner opens fire during an attempted "ambush" on the trail near Dahlonega. Along the section from Springer Mountain to Cooper Gap, Fort Benning soldiers conduct mountain training in Army Ranger operations. The Rangers often direct backpackers to water and shelter. At left, raftsmen approach rapids on the swollen, swiftly flowing Nantahala River in North Carolina.

Clinging mist probably inspired the name Great Smoky Mountains. Twenty-three

onifer-forested peaks of this Tennessee-North Carolina range exceed 6,000 feet.

2.

The Smokies: memories of Cherokee tears

A HIKER deep in the Smokies glimpses infrequently the grandeur around him. Engulfed by mountains and forest, he finds his world shrinking to the path before him—diminished, yet nonetheless fascinating. As the Appalachian Trail wends through the 800-square-mile Great Smoky Mountains National Park, it becomes a green tunnel canopied by a marvelous assortment of trees that range from lowland gums and magnolias to ridgetop conifers. In their shade grow some 1,300 varieties of flowering plants, 350 mosses and liverworts, 230 lichens, and 2,000 kinds of fungus.

But if the botanical story of the Smokies is impressive, the geological story is overwhelming. The mountains were formed by incomprehensibly powerful forces that could crumple a continent as easily as a child might crumple a newspaper.

The rocks of the Smokies are mostly pebbly, sandy, and muddy sediments that filled an arm of the ocean on the site of the present mountains a billion to 600 million years ago. Then about 230 million years ago, great convulsions shook the earth, folding, faulting, and twisting it, and a new mountain system was born—an event geologists call the Appalachian Revolution, which left the rock formations of the Smokies in their present position. Ever since, the mountain system has been under attack by erosion.

A complex chemical and atmospheric interaction covered the mountains with rich soil, which glaciers from the north would have stripped away—as they did in New England—had they not stopped at the Ohio River. As it was, Canadian-zone flora and fauna retreating before the rivers of ice established new footholds high in the Smokies, where they still survive. Because of the glaciers, and the range of elevations, there are

Gravestones of pioneers cast long morning shadows in a churchyard at Cades Cove, Tennessee, within Great Smoky Mountains National Park.

more than 150 kinds of trees now growing in the Smoky Mountains.

The Appalachian Trail enters the Smokies from the southwest by way of a concrete roadway atop Fontana Dam; but we began our hike farther on, at Newfound Gap near the park's center, on a wet afternoon. A thunderstorm—nothing unusual, for the Smokies get as much as 100 inches of rain a year—had washed the forest a few hours before. Mosses, ferns, and trees sparkled, and birds that had taken refuge during the storm were starting to sing again. The puddles underfoot reflected patches of blue sky and green foliage.

Through the Smokies the trail generally follows the Tennessee-North Carolina border. It is well maintained by the National Park Service, so while the mountains are big, the going is fairly easy. In some places we curved around peaks, avoiding a climb over the top, and in others we ascended by switchbacks.

The popularity of the Smoky Mountains soon became apparent. Whereas we had met only one backpacker previously, we encountered a couple of hundred in the three and a half days we took to hike to the northeastern boundary of the park—about 35 miles.

Shelters are likely to be crowded here. The first night out we arrived in a drizzle at Ice Water Springs to find both lean-tos crammed with Boy Scouts. In the gloom they looked like uneasy forest creatures, peering over the edges of the double-decker bunks. Another night we squeezed in with a YMCA group from Connecticut.

The shelters in the Smokies are more confining than the others we had used because each has a fourth side made of heavy wire fencing—to keep out the bears.

Black bears roam the Smokies in considerable numbers—authorities estimate there are about 350 within the park. In the campgrounds the noise of their rummaging in garbage cans resounds nightly. They show up at roadside parking areas to beg handouts, often causing traffic jams. Despite repeated warnings by the Park Service, tourists continue to feed them. Consequently most of the bears in well-traveled parts of the park seem tame, and visitors are often reluctant to believe they can quickly turn grumpy—or furious—when the food is gone.

The Park Service has sound reasons for its rule against feeding the bears. First, of course, is the potential danger. Further, wild animals that become dependent on handouts get lazy and lose the ability to forage for themselves—and suffer with hunger when the tourists leave in the fall.

Although the smallest of North American bears, the black bear is very strong. The adults generally weigh between 200 and 300 pounds and often live more than 15 years. They don't see very well, but have acute senses of smell and hearing. Omniverous, they eat rodents, reptiles, amphibians, fish, and carrion as well as vegetable food. Honey is a favorite treat; a bear will sit and eat his fill from a bee tree, crying piteously all the while from the stings on his unprotected face.

Despite the familiar tale of a long winter's nap in a hollow log, bears don't truly hibernate. They put on extra fat in the fall and sleep through most of the cold weather, but their metabolism and body temperature remain high, and they are easily awakened.

In spring the bear emerges from his den and goes looking for food. With the arrival of summer he sheds his winter coat and finds a mate. A cub arrives the next January or February; often twins are born. Blind, toothless, nearly hairless, the cubs at birth measure less than a foot long and weigh less than a pound. They spend about a year and a half with their mother, avoiding the cantankerous father; he may actually turn cannibal, killing his own offspring if other food is scarce.

Despite the number of bears in the Smokies, hikers on the trail seldom see one; as bold as the roadside bears become, their cousins in the back country generally avoid man and pose little threat except to food supplies and packs, which they methodically tear apart. When we slept outside a shelter, we hung our packs from tree limbs at least eight feet off the ground—choosing limbs that would support the pack but not a bear.

The night we stopped at the Pecks Corner Lean-to, a bear arrived just at supper time. We all crowded into the shelter, slammed the gate, and eyed him as warily as he eyed us. After circling the shelter a couple of times and sniffing us thoroughly, he lumbered away.

A NETWORK of 600 miles of walking trails crisscrosses the park, including the 70-mile segment of the Appalachian Trail. Many of the routes can be hiked easily in a day or less. Late one afternoon near Smokemont Campground, Jill and I ambled down a short nature trail where small signs identify plants along the way. We were puzzled to find some Norway spruces, and later learned how they got here: A forest fire years ago, before the park was established, stripped the trees from Richland Mountain a few miles away. A paper company replanted the mountain with Norway spruce, and it has slowly spread.

On the same walk we watched in amusement while a couple of dozen chattering, skittering chipmunks darted among the fallen leaves with great urgency—though they seemed to have no particular destination.

Another day we made the four-and-a-half-mile round trip to Alum Cave Bluffs, where an overhang of black slate 150 feet high and 300 feet long loomed above us. There we met a hardy young man with one leg in a cast up to his knee. He was in high spirits and determined to reach the top of Mount Le Conte, another three miles.

The route to Alum Cave Bluffs passes over one of the park's curious heath balds, or laurel slicks—or laurel hells, as the mountaineers used to call them—tangles of laurel and rhododendron that are nearly impenetrable except where the path cuts through. Their existence remains unexplained: Why are these parts of the mountain slopes devoid of trees? Some foresters think devastating fires long ago created the clearings, and that the mountain laurel and rhododendron shrubs then sprouted in the burned-over areas before the trees could re-establish themselves.

Equally puzzling are grass balds, mountaintop meadowlands. The Indians may have cleared these originally, perhaps as gathering places for religious ceremonies. Or landslides and violent wind patterns may have erased the ancient tree cover.

One of the most prominent of the Smokies is Mount Guyot, named for the Swiss-born geographer who charted much of this range in the mid-19th century. Without benefit of accurate maps or cleared trails, carrying a fragile, cumbersome barometer and enough food for a week, he struggled alone to the top of almost every peak in the Smokies to determine its elevation by calculations based on atmospheric pressure. His measurements have proved amazingly accurate, usually within a few feet of those made by modern surveying techniques.

Near the summit of Mount Guyot we were above 6,000 feet, and a cool breeze played through the towering balsam and spruce. We descended more than 3,000 feet that day, and the change of climate was dramatic: It was muggy and hot when we reached Davenport Gap, where friends met us with a car.

Transportation arrangements pose a problem for hikers. We usually solved it with two cars, spotting one ahead at our destination, then driving the other to the starting point. It's generally unwise, of course, to leave a car unattended for several days; usually we were able to find someone living near the trail who would let us park in his yard or driveway.

The main route through the park is Newfound Gap Road, which enters on the Tennessee side at Gatlinburg and on the North Carolina side at Cherokee—a name that recalls a bitter period of American history.

The Cherokee Nation once occupied a vast region that covered parts of what are now eight Southern states. Hernando de Soto came upon the Cherokees in 1540 and found them a quiet, agricultural people governed by a loosely knit tribal organization. They lived in sturdy, grass-roofed houses with walls of upright poles interlaced with cane and covered with clay. In the fertile valleys they raised corn, beans, pumpkins, and squash.

During the American Revolution the Cherokees sided with the British against the colonists, but after signing a treaty in 1785 with the new Government they fought alongside the Americans in the War of 1812. Cherokee braves helped Maj. Gen. Andrew Jackson turn the tide against Britain's Creek Indian allies at the Battle of Horseshoe Bend near what is now Alexander City, Alabama.

In 1827 the Cherokees adopted a constitution, and their sovereignty was recognized by the United States. They collected their own taxes for roads and schools, suppressed intemperance and polygamy, and forbade the selling of land to white men.

At least one man of undisputed genius arose from their ranks. Sequoya, an illiterate silversmith who had been crippled in a hunting accident, became intrigued by the white man's ability to "talk on paper" and resolved to devise a system of writing for his own people. After years of lonely work and ridicule, he created a Cherokee alphabet with 85 characters, one for each syllable in the spoken language. A Cherokee child could learn it in only a few months.

For a while the Cherokee civilization flourished. Its boats hauled home-grown cotton to New Orleans for trade; its farms produced cattle, horses, sheep, goats, and hogs; the women made butter and cheese, and wove cloth from cotton and wool; Cherokee innkeepers kept hostelries along well-maintained roads; and almost everyone learned to read and write.

The tribe established a newspaper in 1828—the *Cherokee Phoenix*—just in time to record catastrophe. For when Benjamin Parks stumbled upon his golden nugget in the hills around Dahlonega, the discovery meant the Cherokees' doom. Georgia promptly expropriated the Cherokee lands within her borders, nullified Indian laws and customs, and decreed that no Indian could be a witness in any suit involving a white man.

Farming parcels of 160 acres and mining parcels of 40 acres were carved from the Indians' territory and given away by lottery, with every white Georgian eligible for a ticket.

Later laws ceded every Cherokee family 160 acres, but since an Indian could not defend his rights in court, the gesture had little effect, and in fact his land could be taken by any white man who wanted it. Indians were even forbidden to dig for gold on the land they managed to keep.

In the end, the Cherokees had to move. On May 23, 1836, President Jackson proclaimed a treaty giving the Cherokees two years in which to abandon their homes and resettle 700 miles to the west in what is now Oklahoma. In 1838 Maj. Gen. Winfield Scott arrived to carry out the removal: "The President of the United States has sent me, with a powerful army, to cause you, in obedience to the treaty . . . to join that part of your people who are already established in prosperity on the other side of the Mississippi. . . . The full moon of May is already on the wane, and before another shall have passed away, every Cherokee man, woman, and child must be in motion to join their brethren in the far West."

During that summer at least 5,000 Cherokees journeyed down the Tennessee and Ohio Rivers to the Mississippi, where they disembarked and began the long walk across Arkansas. In the heat many sickened and died, so Cherokee leaders asked that further removal await cooler weather, and that chiefs be allowed to lead their people overland. In the fall the remaining 13,000 set out.

"It was like the march of an army, regiment after regiment," wrote one historian, "the wagons in the center, the officers along the line and the horsemen on the flanks and at the rear." One of the soldiers assigned to escort them wrote of the experience 50 years later. "On the morning of November 17th we encountered a terrific sleet and snow storm with freezing temperatures and from that day until we reached the end of the fateful journey on March the 26th 1839, the sufferings of the Cherokees were awful. The trail of the exiles was a trail of death. They had to sleep in the wagons and on the ground without fire. And I have known as many as twenty-two of them to die in one night of pneumonia due to ill treatment, cold, and exposure."

All told, 4,000 died. The Cherokees called it the Trail of Tears.

There remained in the mountains about a thousand refugees who had fled when the roundups began. Rather than hunt them down, General Scott—whose troops were needed in Florida against the Seminoles—agreed to let them stay if they would turn over to him one of their number wanted for murder. They complied, and it is their descendants who today populate the Cherokee Indian Reservation in the eastern foothills of the Smokies. The reservation's principal settlement is the town of Cherokee, North Carolina.

We made the mistake of trying to drive down Cherokee's main street on the Fourth of July, a day when some 25,000 automobiles were heading into the national park through this point of entry. The brutal sun pushed tempers and radiators to the boiling point.

Curio shops lined the main street, catering to visitors searching for souvenirs; tourist children crowding the sidewalks clutched toy tepees, plastic bears, and bows and arrows.

But there are places in Cherokee that offer authentic, carefully fashioned Cherokee art and craft objects. One of these is the Qualla Arts and Crafts Mutual, a cooperative formed by the Cherokees in 1946 with the help of the Bureau of Indian Affairs. In a low, modern stone building near the edge of town, shelves and counters display stone sculpture, woodcarvings, baskets, and beadwork. Both design and workmanship are of high quality. The baskets are intricately woven of white oak, river cane, and honeysuckle vines, patterned with dyes made from vegetables and roots. Many of the carvings portray animals of the region, especially bears, foxes, and opossums.

Mrs. Betty DuPree, the part-Cherokee manager, told us how the cooperative works and the purpose it tries to fulfill. "Indian artists who are members of the cooperative bring us their work; we buy it from them—for whatever they ask, if possible—and then sell it. From the profits we pay dividends twice a year to the 120 members who are producing work, and Christmas bonuses to all 265 members."

I N THE MEMBERS' GALLERY adjoining the sales room, a one-man show by John Julius Wilnoty was on display. Gleaming on glass shelves beneath bright lights were small, complex sculptures of human and animal figures intricately intertwined, their limbs contorted and dissolving into bodies of snakes and imaginary creatures. A carving titled "Primitive Hunter" caught an Indian man and a bear locked in a death struggle, the bear snarling in panic and rage, the hunter coolly disdainful and clearly in control. The show's centerpiece was "Eagle Dancer," a 29-inch-high cherrywood sculpture of a feathered dancer frozen in midwhirl.

We found John Wilnoty at his home a few miles outside Cherokee. "To see me you wouldn't think I was anything but a bum," he greeted us, smiling shyly. Wearing old jeans and a tattered Army jacket, he leaned against the fender of a car as he talked. Dogs, cats, chickens, and dark-eyed children shared the dusty yard.

It's a wonder John is alive to be carving. A childhood injury led to sleeping epilepsy, an ailment for which he must still take medication regularly to prevent his dropping off to sleep unintentionally and at dangerous moments. Later he accidentally shot himself with a pistol. He has run chisels into his hands several times.

He combines a confidence in Indian medicine men—one of whom, he insists, correctly diagnosed the sleeping epilepsy before the white doctors —with a devout, fundamentalist Baptist faith. "I carve because that's the talent God gave me," he said. "I was lucky I found it.

"I just carve what I see in the stone," he continued, leaning against the car and casually scratching on a work in progress. He roams the nearby mountains looking for suitable pipestone to carve, and makes his own sculpturing tools from old knives and chisels. "I work on a piece for a while, maybe put it aside for a couple of years, then study it and carve some more."

Raymond Grant, another descendant of the Cherokees who stayed behind, was costumed in feathers and beads and busy dancing for tips and posing for snapshots when we came upon him at the entrance to an amusement park gift shop.

As he performed, his wife Eleanor strung beads, seated on the tailgate of their well-worn station wagon. Their four-year-old son Ernest, wearing a war bonnet and beaded chaps, played with toy trucks in the gravel nearby.

With his bottomless brown eyes and curly black hair, Ernest often steals the show; women tend to fuss over him. Before a recent trip to the barber, his hair was long enough to cause occasional misidentification: "I ain't no girl," he told one visitor emphatically.

Eleanor encourages him to dance, but not too strongly. "If I push him, he'll hate it," she says.

Three teen-age boys were working with Raymond and a fourth played the drums as they demonstrated traditional Cherokee dances. After a spattering of applause and the clink of a few coins in the basket, Raymond gathered tourist children onto the wooden platform and taught them a couple of steps. Later he and Ernest posed with the youngsters as parents' cameras clicked.

Toward evening, as the crowd thinned, the Grants prepared to leave for home. Warm, open people, they had become our friends during the long afternoon, and we gladly accepted their invitation to supper.

We followed them about four miles into the reservation to their rented four-room, cinder-block, hillside home. A well-tended garden clung to the sloping back yard. "Cabbage, beans, corn, tomatoes, mustard, potatoes," said Eleanor with pride. "It's the first real garden I've had." Two German shepherd puppies, penned up all day, yelped and wagged for joy at being set free. Inside, a cat greeted us with a yawn.

"Indians own all the land on the reservation," said Raymond, as Eleanor started preparing supper, "but the Government holds the deeds in trust. We can sell to each other—with the approval of the tribal council—or we can lease our land to whites, but no Indian land can be sold to whites.

."The tribal council," he added, "has 12 members elected by the Indians every two years, plus a chief and vice-chief elected for four years. The reservation"—about 56,000 acres and 5,000 people—"is run like a small city. We have our own police force and fire department, and—in town—water and sewage systems. The schools are starting to teach the Cherokee language again. It wasn't too long ago that any child caught speaking Cherokee in a classroom had his mouth washed out with soap."

Over fried chicken, potatoes, corn, peas, rice, and flat "fry bread" cooked in a skillet, Raymond reminisced about his tour in the Navy as a young man—"I fell off a bridge in Genoa and broke practically every bone in the left side of my body"—and how he met Eleanor in Cherokee about six years ago. There were in-law problems, so the newlyweds moved to Atlanta, where Raymond finally got a job as a truck driver.

"Those were bad times," Eleanor remembered. "It was months before Raymond could find work. There were usually beans on the table then, and bologna—reservation steak."

"Last summer," said Raymond, "I worked in Atlanta all week and then on Friday nights I'd drive up here to Cherokee and spend the weekend performing, then drive back to Atlanta in time for work Monday morning. It got to be too much, so in September we moved here permanently."

"When we first moved in," Eleanor added, "we had that water heater in the corner and three sleeping bags. Everything else was in Atlanta."

Raymond and Eleanor supplement their income by stringing beads and making moccasins in the off-season. "We've sat up far into the night stringing those things," said Eleanor with a grimace. "We get 23 cents for beading and sewing a pair of child's moccasins that will sell in the shops for two or three dollars."

Raymond would like to run for the council someday. "I need to get closer personally to the people first—we've only been back here a year, and people will have to know and trust me before they'd vote for me. I'd try to see some changes made. In the prices the gift shops pay for handicrafts, for instance. And better housing for the people."

After coffee, Eleanor rose. "Well," she said, "let's go to the clogging."

We looked blank.

"The dance," she said.

At a drive-in back on the highway The Cherokee Three—a drummer and two guitarists with amplifiers—were thumping out country tunes. A semicircle of cars in the parking lot faced a wooden platform about 12 feet square. Every second car seemed to have a grandmother inside and a child or two on the hood. Men and women leaned against fenders or stood in clusters to watch the cloggers on the platform.

To a strong and steady beat, the dancers whirled and stomped. Clogging is a happy, exuberant dance, part hopscotch, part jitterbug, part rain dance. It requires no partner, and men, women, and children—singly and in pairs—crowded the platform. The hollow thumping of their feet on the boards echoed off the cars, while moths, attracted to the lights, seemed to swirl to the same rhythm. The Cherokees, suddenly free and joyous, a smile on every face, danced long into the night.

On a rainy July day a trail-wide puddle mirrors trees and tall rhododendrons as Jill and Ron backpack through the Great Smoky Mountains.

Ready to resume a 70-mile hike in the Great Smokies, Boy Scout Troop 200 of Nashville lines up at the New Ice Water Spring Lean-to. On the trail the boys kept sharp watch for poisonous snakes, such as the northern copperhead at left.

Black bears abound in the Great Smoky Mountains. One night a bold one made the Scouts thankful they were inside a shelter. Scenting food, the beast lunged again and again at a chain-link fence across the front of the lean-to before wandering off.

"I carve because that's the talent God gave me. I was lucky I found it."

"Old Mother," shown at left 1½ times actual size, looks up from her nursing infant with an expression "so compelling," said one observer, "that the stone seems to breathe." Such vitality helped gain Cherokee sculptor John Julius Wilnoty nationwide recognition. Because the effects of a childhood accident prevented him from holding a job, he began carving in the early 1960's — teaching himself — so he could support his family.

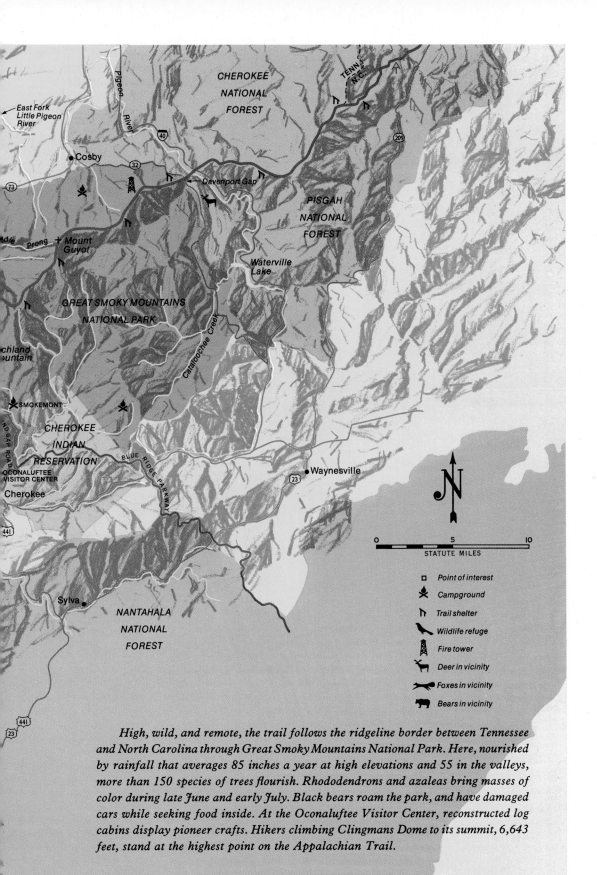

East Fork
Little Pigeon
River

CHEROKEE
NATIONAL
FOREST

Pigeon River

40

Cosby

32

73

Davenport Gap

PISGAH
NATIONAL
FOREST

209

TENN.
N.C.

Mount
Guyot

Prong

Waterville
Lake

GREAT SMOKY MOUNTAINS
NATIONAL PARK

Cataloochee Creek

chland
untain

SMOKEMONT

CHEROKEE
INDIAN
RESERVATION

ND GAP ROAD

BLUE RIDGE PARKWAY

OCONALUFTEE
VISITOR CENTER

Cherokee

441

Waynesville

23

Sylva

NANTAHALA
NATIONAL
FOREST

441

23

N

0   5   10
STATUTE MILES

☐   Point of interest
⚜   Campground
⌂   Trail shelter
⟶   Wildlife refuge
⚒   Fire tower
⚲   Deer in vicinity
⚲   Foxes in vicinity
🐻   Bears in vicinity

High, wild, and remote, the trail follows the ridgeline border between Tennessee
and North Carolina through Great Smoky Mountains National Park. Here, nourished
by rainfall that averages 85 inches a year at high elevations and 55 in the valleys,
more than 150 species of trees flourish. Rhododendrons and azaleas bring masses of
color during late June and early July. Black bears roam the park, and have damaged
cars while seeking food inside. At the Oconaluftee Visitor Center, reconstructed log
cabins display pioneer crafts. Hikers climbing Clingmans Dome to its summit, 6,643
feet, stand at the highest point on the Appalachian Trail.

Fourth of July traffic jam (top) means a temporary business boom in Cherokee, North Carolina. Outside a gift shop, Raymond Grant (right) performs tribal dances for tips. Hatband slogans worn by two visitors to the Cherokee reservation (above) struck Dick as ironic: "Where else would an Indian —the original American—want to go?"

"The reason
I came back was—
I came home."

"If there's something I see another man doing, I don't see no reason why I can't do it."

Cherokees at home: His day of dancing over, Raymond Grant joins his wife Eleanor in the kitchen to peel potatoes while she fries chicken. At left, they cut sumac saplings to use as bean poles and tomato stakes. Indian handicrafts bring in some money in winter—but not much: A beaded bracelet (right) that takes more than an hour to make sells for about 60 cents wholesale.

3.

The Wilderness Road and Iron Mountain

WITH ANTICIPATION and some apprehension, I left my companions to begin a solitary five-day hike in Tennessee. Anticipation, because almost everyone who hikes seems to agree that one of the chief rewards is solitude—the pervading silence and absolute independence that come with being on your own for a few days in the woods. Apprehension, because most hiking authorities warn that the hazards of solitary wilderness travel outweigh the rewards.

I didn't make the decision lightly. A pamphlet published by the Appalachian Trail Conference—*Suggestions for Appalachian Trail Users*—ends a list of precautions with "*. . . and as a final monition, do not travel alone.*" Colin Fletcher, author of several books on hiking, writes: "Many experienced outdoorsmen—and all responsible hiking organizations—contend that the greatest danger in wilderness travel is . . . walking alone."

A lone hiker in the wilderness can find himself in serious trouble should he get lost, sprain an ankle, or suffer a snakebite or the sting of a poisonous insect.

Still, I told myself, more people are injured each year by falling in bathtubs than are bitten by snakes. And of the 1,100 or so who are bitten, only about a dozen die. The odds must be good that I would not be one of the dozen. As for getting lost, I decided that some common-sense precautions at the start of the trip—letting others know exactly where I was going, taking good maps and a compass, and being certain I knew how to use them—would help ensure that I didn't go astray.

But my principal rationale was that a writer needs to know his subject well, and I wanted to experience as many aspects of wilderness travel—including solitude—as I could. So, without doubting the soundness of the

Dewdrops bejewel a budding branch in Virginia. The hikers found that dew traced delicate patterns on grass and trees almost every night.

advice, I decided to ignore it for just a few days and to set out by myself.

As it turned out, there was less time alone than I expected. I encountered other people on the trail and at shelters, stopped off at farmhouses and villages, made side trips for interviews. But in between were some of the loneliest, quietest, and most peaceful days I have ever known.

Driving from Elizabethton toward my starting point, Watauga Dam, I followed one of the oldest roads in the mountains, blazed in 1775 by Daniel Boone. When Richard Henderson, a retired North Carolina judge, acquired land for a new colony in Kentucky and Tennessee, he commissioned Boone to establish a route settlers could follow. On previous hunting and exploring trips Boone had ranged up the Watauga River Valley and through the site of present-day Elizabethton. The road he marked to Kentucky pushed on through Cumberland Gap, and for a generation it was the most important road westward. For the first groups the going wasn't easy, as an excerpt from a journal makes clear: "Wednesday.... Breaks away fair & we go on down the valey & camp on indian Creek we had this Creek to cross maney times & very Bad Banks Abrams Saddel turned & the load all fell in we got out this Eavening and kill two Deer."

First called Boone's Trace, the route later became famous as the Wilderness Road.

The Bad Banks are pretty much a thing of the past now, at least along the Watauga. The Tennessee Valley Authority dammed the river in 1948 with 3.5 million cubic yards of earth and rock fill. All told, 33 major dams check the Tennessee River and its tributaries, and their powerhouses generate electricity for farms, factories, office buildings, and homes.

On a bluff high above Watauga Dam I shouldered my pack and set off toward Damascus, Virginia, 37 miles away. I caught an occasional glimpse of the long, narrow reservoir as I hiked around it, down ridges and over gentle hills of the million-acre Cherokee National Forest.

I overtook a birdwatcher who had strolled out from his home nearby, but he turned out to be more interested in discussing binoculars than birds: His own were magnificent, and he seemed quite disappointed in the small, scuffed pair of field glasses hanging around my neck. He did identify for me the splendid cardinal flowers that burst in fiery clusters beside the trail.

At one point that day I met a box turtle. When it saw me, it quickly retreated into its shell. Gingerly I picked it up and examined it; I had never touched a large turtle before. Its scribed, high-domed shell was very hard, and the front and rear edges were surprisingly sharp. I carefully placed it under a bush well off the path.

Farther on, the trail crossed the scene of a fire that occurred in April 1963. The blaze spread from burning debris and consumed 2,800 acres of trees and brush. Three converted World War II bombers repeatedly flew in through the turbulent mountain air to drop chemical retardants, and 200 fire fighters joined the battle. Two of the men were trapped when the fire jumped the spot where they were operating their bulldozers. They cleared an area with their machines and safely waited it out, surrounded by raging flame and acrid smoke. The fire was finally halted, after three days, just half a mile from the little Tennessee town of Butler.

As I crossed the burned-over area a lush growth of weeds soaked by the previous night's rain reached to my waist, whipped my bare legs, and hid the trail. Burned trees thrust blackened skeletons above the undergrowth. Blackberry thorns caught at my clothing, as if determined to hold me back. I remembered a tale that some kinds of snakes like to lie in wait for their prey underneath bushes, and I half expected at every step to feel the strike of small, sharp fangs against my leg. The next trailside shelter was a welcome sight.

After a solitary supper I followed a bee that was working late, moving from cluster to cluster of pink, inch-wide mountain laurel blossoms, to a rocky outcrop behind the shelter. Far below me was Butler, a community of about 350 families scattered over the foothills beside Watauga Lake. A dog's barking drifted up to me, surprisingly distinct in the quiet evening air, and then came the sound of hammering. At dusk a church bell began to toll its invitation. And so on Sunday, freshly scrubbed, I accepted by attending the eleven o'clock service at the Cobbs Creek Baptist Church.

The Reverend David Cunningham, tall and tanned, welcomed me along with the rest of a congregation of about 50 in the spacious, airy church. I was glad I had spruced up, for everyone else was in proper Sunday garb. The women looked more comfortable than the men, whose neckties obviously were an unaccustomed constraint. The men shared the common mark of those who wear hats while working under a harsh sun: stark white foreheads contrasting with deeply tanned faces.

Sunbeams streamed through open windows onto wooden Communion railings around the altar. We sang "Shall We Gather at the River," and Mr. Cunningham preached a sermon on *The Unimportance of Appearances*—with a glance at my budding beard—blessed us with a short benediction, and dismissed us into the sunshine.

There was no service of baptism that day, but I learned that few churches still follow what was once the popular Southern practice of baptizing believers in creeks and rivers—to the disappointment of one old gentleman I met. His elderly neighbor, he said, loved baptisms more than anything. "All the boys in town would come down to the creek just to hear Granny holler," he told me. "She'd holler a while and then she'd faint."

MY LEAN-TO above Butler was on the boundary of a whippoorwill's territory, and he called out his name all night long. For the first hour it was lovely; after that I began to lose my enthusiasm for his song. People of Appalachia say the number of times a whippoorwill calls equals the number of years of freedom left to a bachelor. But sometimes the bird exaggerates: Naturalist John Burroughs heard one call 1,478 times, with only a brief pause.

In the cinder blocks of Iron Mountain Shelter some bumblebees had built a home. Sprawled on my unrolled sleeping bag, my boots off and a cup of coffee in hand, I listened to their soft humming and watched their coming and going. From the spring nearby came a distinctive sound: the beating wings of a hummingbird that flitted among the laurel blossoms.

A mouse on a ledge under the roof apparently couldn't decide what sort of threat I posed. Whenever I looked at him he stopped his scampering and regarded me cautiously, his big ears turned toward me like cupped antennas. In the night I heard him squeaking indignantly inside my pack as he searched for the food I had hidden in a zippered pocket.

On top of Iron Mountain, just to the left of the trail, is the grave of a hermit who dwelt here some 40 years. At first glance his monument looks like the chimney of a burned-out cabin. It bears this inscription: "Uncle Nick Grindstaff. Born Dec. 26, 1851—Died July 22, 1923. Lived alone, suffered alone, died alone."

His life story was told in a long poem written in 1926 by Adam M. Daugherty, "Poet Laureate of Johnson County."

> ... *Nick was left at the age of three,*
> *Left to an orphan's fate was he,*
> *Left in a world of sin and woe,*
> *No father or mother to show*
> *His little feet which way to go....*

Nick grew up and led an uneventful life until, on a trip to the West at the age of 26, he was robbed and beaten. Disillusioned, he became a recluse and sought a spot for a home on Iron Mountain.

> *No love could turn his mind agog,*
> *Unless it was, perhaps his dog....*
> *A fine work ox he always kept,*
> *That roved the mountain while Nick slept ...*
> *And stood still as a gentle fawn,*
> *So Nick could put the harness on.*

A friend named Sam came for a visit one day and was astonished to see a rattlesnake in the cabin.

> *Then Sam said, "Let me kill it quick,"*
> *"No, no, Sam, that's my pet," said Nick....*
> *He roamed up there for forty years,*
> *Under the heavens' chandeliers ...*
> *And thus he slept within his rights,*
> *Fourteen thousand, four hundred nights....*

A farmer from the valley stopped by Nick's cabin one day in 1923 and found him dead. His little dog was beside him, and it grew so fierce when men came to bury Nick that it had to be destroyed.

On the northwest slope of Cross Mountain the trail led me up the gravel driveway of Lester and Pearl Osborne, who have had hikers trudging past their house, down a lane, and through their barnyard for 12 years. I visited with diminutive, white-haired Mrs. Osborne on the front porch.

"Lester and I are both from North Carolina," she told me, "but we moved around out West a lot while Lester worked on construction projects. In '59 we came here to settle down and farm.

"We have about 250 acres. Lester breeds cattle and has a plot of tobacco, and I have my garden. I freeze and can all my own vegetables and make jellies and grape juice. In our basement are jars of pickles, jellies, and vegetables. We butcher beef out of our own herd. And in the woods there are blueberries and raspberries. It's a good life."

I asked how she liked having hikers underfoot all the time.

"They're good people," she said. "We've never had any trouble with them. There have been more this summer than ever before. Once in a while one asks for water, or if he can sleep in the barn.

"The cows still aren't used to seeing people with packs on. But only squirrel hunters and large groups of boys really scare them. Those are the only people who give us any problems. The youngsters don't understand about the gates, and a lot of the squirrel hunters don't seem to care."

What would happen now that the trail is coming under the protection of the National Trails System Act and the Department of Interior is acquiring permanent rights-of-way?

"They're moving it off our place sometime this summer," she said. "Back down the road a ways where it'll go through the woods.

"We're going to miss those hikers. Up here alone, it's nice having people coming through. They stop and talk if we're out and around."

As I sat by my fire that evening, almost hypnotized by the embers, a hearty, bare-chested young man walked up. His first words—"How's the water situation?"—reflected a chief concern of all hikers.

His name was Bruce Ackerman; he reported that he was from Rockville, Maryland, planned to enter the Massachusetts Institute of Technology in the fall, and had spent the previous summer hiking 520 miles of the trail in New England. On the present trip he was going from Damascus, Virginia, to Springer Mountain.

He had one piece of good news that had passed up the trail grapevine while I was exploring nearby communities. Thor, the lost Labrador retriever whose owner we had met at the beginning of our trek, had wandered up to a ranger's cabin; so the family from Cincinnati had been reunited.

As we talked, I asked him just why he hiked. He thought a minute and shrugged. "I like the views," he said, and let it go at that. His feet never bothered him, he said, but his pack got uncomfortable: One of his shoulders was slightly lower than the other so the pack didn't ride evenly.

Before turning in, he taught me a handy trick: He mixed a package of Jell-O in a small pot and set it in the spring with a rock on the lid. Next morning it made a delicious addition to breakfast.

Later that day a grouse hen tried to lure me away from her chicks by feigning injury. As the chicks scurried one way, she went the other, dragging one wing and crying plaintively. But she gave herself away by stopping every few feet and looking back to see whether I was following.

Damascus sits astride the trail near the Virginia-Tennessee line; the route goes right down Laurel Avenue, the main street, past stores, garages, and service stations.

There was already a small community here in 1821 when Henry Mock established a gristmill on the creek, giving the town its first name: Mock's Mill. Married three times, the father of 30, doughty Henry lived well into his nineties.

In 1886 Brig. Gen. John D. Imboden, who had served as one of Robert E. Lee's chief lieutenants, bought most of the town from Henry and changed the name to Damascus. "The presence of these mountains," he wrote, "with their vast stores of iron ore, manganese and timber, their splendid water supply, the proximity of coal fields, led to the selection of this spot as the very best in the United States for a modern 'Damascus,' destined to become as famous, we believe, as its ancient namesake in Asia as a steel producing city."

It turned out that practically the only iron in Iron Mountain was in its name, and General Imboden's prophecy failed. But the town is near the border of the new Mount Rogers National Recreation Area, encompassing Virginia's highest mountain, and a burgeoning tourist industry may yet give Damascus the prosperity it missed.

Many long-distance hikers who plan to pass through Damascus mail packages to themselves in advance, in care of General Delivery. So their first stop in town is usually the new brick post office.

Postmaster Paschal Grindstaff (unrelated to the hermit) has been looking after hikers and their packages for 15 years. He reserves a special shelf for hikers' mail, and he showed me a large folder of correspondence, mostly letters notifying him of expected arrival dates in Damascus and notes thanking him for holding packages or forwarding mail. One note, from a young hiker's mother, said, "If he looks as if he needs a haircut, will you please direct him to a barber?"

As I was browsing through the folder, a tall, striking woman entered the post office. "That's Mrs. Van McQueen," said the postmaster, "a widow who takes in hikers. You might want to stay a night at her place."

I found Mrs. McQueen's large white house, shaded by huge maples, on Laurel Avenue, its porch barely five yards from the Appalachian Trail. Only that day a new granddaughter had arrived, so the house was bustling with excitement, but Mrs. McQueen took time to visit. "My cousin across the street took in hikers for many years," she said. "I lived with her for some time after my husband died, but she too died just recently, so I've moved back into my old home. It's too big for just me so I decided to continue the tradition and offer lodging to hikers. They're wonderful people.

"Most of them have a long bath first, then go to the self-service laundry, then redo their packs, with the food and all."

She was concerned about one man for whom she was holding letters and a package. She'd been told by another hiker that he'd be there no later than Sunday, and now it was Tuesday. "I'm sure he's sick," she said.

Her bathtub was indeed a luxury, and one of her spare beds all a hiker could ask. The charge for the night was four dollars.

The mountains around Damascus have long been a rich source of handicrafts. To a great extent the early settlers had to make what they needed or do without. Mountain craftsmen learned to fashion articles both useful and handsome — furniture, pottery, quilts, musical instruments.

Many of the traditional skills and designs were nearly lost when mail-order catalogues and inexpensive cotton prints began to find their way to secluded mountain communities. Old recipes for dyes, patterns for woven fabrics, knowledge of the properties of various native woods — such lore almost disappeared, along with the looms that had been gathering dust in cabin corners.

Then in the 1930's and 1940's a revival began, and today an impressive stream of craft articles flows out of the mountains. Appalachian baskets, pottery, ironwork, braided rugs, woven goods, dolls and other toys, dulcimers, jewelry, quilts, and wood carvings can be bought not only in the mountains and nearby towns but also in most large cities. The Southern Highland Handicraft Guild of Asheville, North Carolina, organized in 1930, helps to train craftsmen and market their work.

I made a short detour from Damascus to Laurel Bloomery, Tennessee, to visit the Iron Mountain Stoneware factory, which has been producing stoneware since 1965. Partly to escape the turmoil and high costs of urban America, partly to take advantage of the traditional handwork interest and aptitude of the Southern mountaineers, Nancy Patterson and Albert Mock settled on Laurel Bloomery for the factory site. Cooperating with the U. S. Department of Labor, the owners hired unemployed people of the community and trained them in the needed skills. More than 400 applied for the initial 15 positions. Today the company has about 65 employees, and its distinctive stoneware is sold nationwide through such firms as Georg Jensen of New York.

Design, production, and management responsibilities are now shared by Nancy Patterson, her husband Joe Lamb, and her sister Sally Patterson.

Mrs. Lamb is well pleased with her decision to locate the factory in the Tennessee mountains. "Our workers have a deep interest in their jobs," she said. "We have a marvelous team of dedicated individuals."

Sally has helped organize an art curriculum in the Damascus Elementary School. She is a perceptive observer of the mountain people. "It's very difficult to teach art to the children if they can't start until the age of 9 or 10," she said. "They learn from their parents to think in traditional ways, to do things the way their fathers and grandfathers did them. This is good for passing on traditional crafts—the youngsters don't deviate from the accepted way—but to teach them to do abstract things we must start their art training when they are very young, and then continue it."

I DECIDED to extend my side trip to Kingsport, Tennessee, to have dinner with Stanley A. Murray. Chairman of the Appalachian Trail Conference, he is largely responsible for the new system of national trails; he helped to draft the legislation and to shepherd it through Congress. A dark-haired native of Maine, short but with the powerful physique of a long-time hiker, he works as a chemical engineer for Eastman Kodak in Kingsport.

"I started hiking in the Smokies when I was stationed down here with the Army," he said. "In 1949 I took the job with Tennessee Eastman, and joined a hiking club." He was elected to his first three-year term as ATC chairman in 1961 and has been re-elected four times.

He has obviously given much thought to the trail. "In 2,000 miles there should be plenty of variety—easy stretches for the older people and beginners, tough sections for the experienced and conditioned. Suppose you were a skier or golfer. Would you want every slope easy enough for a beginner, or every golf course built just for amateurs? Of course not.

"There's a tendency for that to happen to the trail. Someone goes out and hikes part of it. He comes in and says to the ranger, 'That was kind of tough,' so the ranger goes out and levels it a bit. That encourages people to try it who wouldn't have attempted the tougher version; but one of them comes in and says, 'That was kind of tough.' And so on.

"The trail must be more than a place to walk. Its environment is what's important—the richly varied Appalachian mountains and forests."

I asked Stan what part of the trail was his favorite. "Well," he said, "that's not hard to answer. There's a ten-and-a-half-mile stretch along the Tennessee-North Carolina border between Carvers Gap and Highway 19E. It starts on the eastern shoulder of Roan Mountain, and many people say it's the most beautiful section of the trail. Don't miss it."

I timed my visit to Roan Mountain to coincide with the annual rhododendron spectacle in June. I arrived by car, joining the heavy traffic that inched toward the parking lots high on the mountainside.

Nature's floral display more than made up for the inconveniences of the pilgrimage. From a distance the slopes appeared to be blanketed in pink; as I drew closer I saw that every rhododendron was in full bloom.

I lingered for several hours, then turned my back on the crowds and hiked across Carvers Gap and up Round Bald. When I had crossed the summit, I was alone in Stan's favorite section. And I understood his preference. For the next ten miles the trail winds across treeless ridges offering one panorama after another as mountains spill away to every horizon. The grass around me waved lazily in the soft breeze; the meadow was alive with juncos and bright with four-petaled bluets, the tiny blue flowers that some call Quaker maids, or innocence. Outcroppings of boulders served as platforms for occasional cloud-watching.

Before I rejoined Dick and Jill at Shenandoah National Park, I made still another solitary hike—this time in the Jefferson National Forest of Virginia, walking from the mouth of Dismal Creek to Pearisburg. In 25 miles I met only one person: a fisherman, nearly engulfed by extra-large waders. I spent a night at a shelter so new the fireplace had never been used, and not a single name or comment had been inscribed on the walls.

I had arrived in midafternoon, so I spread my damp towel on a log in the sun. A chipmunk, obviously accustomed to using the log as a thoroughfare, suddenly came hurtling along it. With furious backpedaling he managed to stop just short of the towel; then he peered curiously at it, over at me, back at the towel, and abruptly bolted back the way he had come.

Next morning a flock of small white butterflies entertained me for half an hour as they huddled in the air and then fluttered about uncertainly.

Late in the afternoon from Angels Rest, 2,000 sheer feet above Pearisburg, I watched two hawks circling on motionless wings. They seemed to soar in spite of themselves, so effortlessly did they fly. My binoculars brought their glinting eyes close to mine, and the details of their sleek, efficient feathers. In great spirals they moved far down the valley.

I sat in the sun and watched the hawks, and saw New River curving past Pearisburg, and the solitude was good.

Baton poised, majorette Kawana Sams stands ready to lead the annual Rhododendron Festival parade through Elizabethton, Tennessee.

Hearkening to the skirl of bag-pipes, N. J. MacDonald (right), president of the Grandfather Mountain Highland Games and Gathering of the Clans, wears a traditional tweed jacket and Clan MacDonald tartan tie. Members of 132 clans from 30 states and several other lands — including Scotland — compete in dancing, music, and games during the weekend pageant, held yearly near Linville, North Carolina. With a Highland air, Pipe Major James R. Ross leads the Clan Munro during the Parade of the Tartans. Kilted competitors grapple in a Celtic wrestling match.

"The Scot kind of
loves himself. Give him
the least opportunity
and he'll tell you
how wonderful we are."

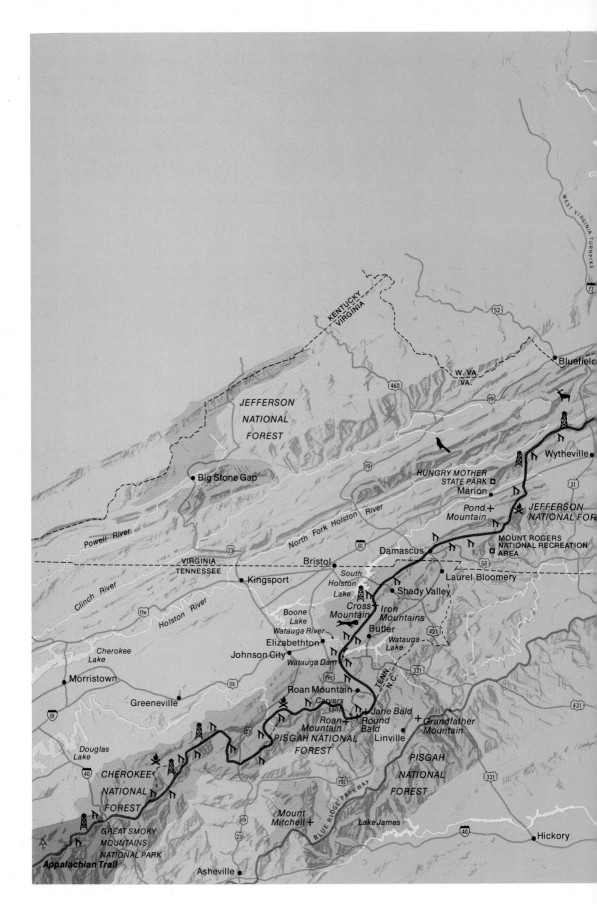

Appalachian Trail

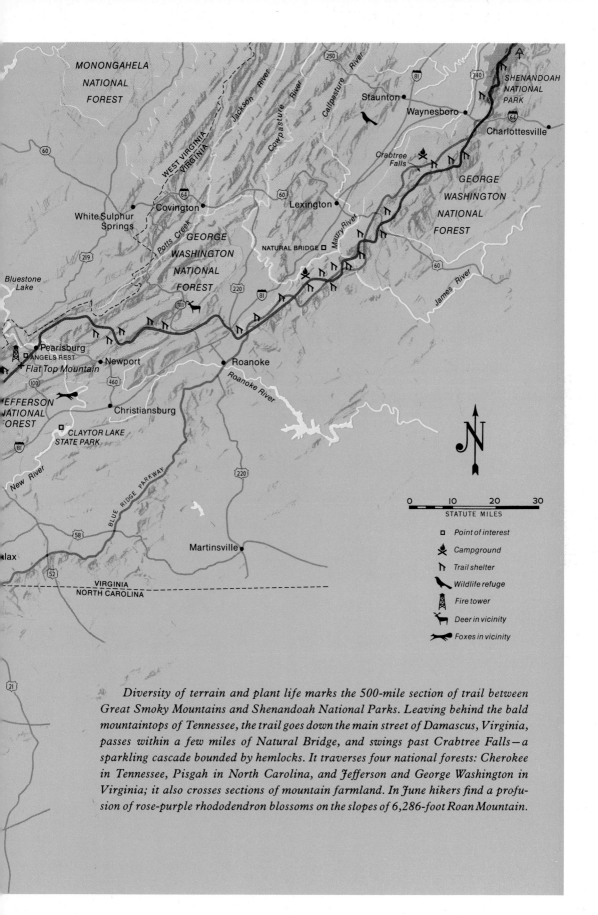

Diversity of terrain and plant life marks the 500-mile section of trail between Great Smoky Mountains and Shenandoah National Parks. Leaving behind the bald mountaintops of Tennessee, the trail goes down the main street of Damascus, Virginia, passes within a few miles of Natural Bridge, and swings past Crabtree Falls—a sparkling cascade bounded by hemlocks. It traverses four national forests: Cherokee in Tennessee, Pisgah in North Carolina, and Jefferson and George Washington in Virginia; it also crosses sections of mountain farmland. In June hikers find a profusion of rose-purple rhododendron blossoms on the slopes of 6,286-foot Roan Mountain.

"The hikers are good people — they always shut the gates."

Sheep on the way to pasture bound through a meadow on Pond Mountain in southern Virginia. Both sheep and cattle graze the region's slopes. On a 250-acre farm in Shady Valley, Tennessee, cattleman Lester Osborne raises Hereford breeding stock. In his feed shed (right), Les pours salt into a bucket for the herd. He spent his younger days as a structural iron worker on jobs in the West. "You know," Les reflected, "usually the most contented people are those who never leave their hometown. Whereas me, there's never been a place I been I wouldn't want to go back to."

Judges grade contestants for the crown of Miss Rhododendron, considering grace, poise, and beauty as the girls turn slowly on the stage of Cloudland High School in Roan Mountain Village, Tennessee. Announcement of the contest's winner highlights the Rhododendron Festival, held each June to celebrate the blooming of rhododendrons on the mountain. At right, Nancy Luntsford of Johnson City receives congratulations from fellow contestants after her selection. Before the ceremony, a man in the audience naps on a grassy slope of Roan Mountain, where the new queen accepts her crown.

Clouds soften morning sunlight at the summit of Round Bald (above), one of a series of grassy, treeless mountaintops in Tennessee. Sampling wild strawberries, Jill rambles through a dense berry patch on Jane Bald. "After a damp, sleepless night," she said, "the fog began blowing away, and we found fields and fields of ripe, red strawberries. Hiking schedules just fall apart during berry season."

"We feasted all morning
on ripe, red, wild strawberries."

4.

Shenandoah: daughter of the stars

"SOMETHING HIDDEN. Go and find it. Go and look behind the Ranges — Something lost . . . and waiting for you. . . ." Rudyard Kipling hinted in "The Explorer" at the mysterious magnet that draws men across mountains to the unknown.

Men have been probing the Appalachians since the days of de Soto. The mountains' name came from that of the Appalachees, a tribe of Indians the Spanish adventurer found living on the Gulf of Mexico.

One of the most unusual expeditions to cross the Blue Ridge took place in 1716. With Alexander Spotswood, the young bachelor governor of colonial Virginia, in command, a party of about 50 friends, rangers, servants, and Indian guides reconnoitered through a gap in the mountains to the Shenandoah Valley. It was a leisurely, gentlemanly undertaking. In high spirits, like a group of college boys on holiday, the party set out from Germanna on the Rapidan River on August 29 — getting a late start that first day, and traveling only three miles.

Spotswood's young aide, John Fontaine, kept a diary of the trip: "We made great fires, and supped, and drank good punch," he wrote. They slept on the ground and awoke "with pains in our bones." Several horses had strayed during the night, and it took much of the day to round them up.

Next day Fontaine went hunting: "I saw a deer, and shot him from my horse, but the horse threw me a terrible fall and ran away; we ran after, and with a great deal of difficulty got him again; but we could not find the deer I had shot, and we lost ourselves, and it was two hours before we could come upon the track of our company." Hornets stung the horses and "did a little damage, but afforded a great deal of diversion."

Dream Lake reflects stalactites in Luray Caverns, Virginia. Water seeping through cracks in dolomite carved these chambers millenniums ago. Mineral-laden droplets continue to form the calcite "icicles."

On September 5 they crested the Blue Ridge, crossing what would later become the Appalachian Trail, beheld the broad Shenandoah Valley, and "drank King George's health, and all the Royal Family's, at the very top of the Appalachian Mountains." The next night, camped on the banks of the Shenandoah River—which they called the Euphrates—they celebrated again. "We had a good dinner, and after it we got the men together, and loaded all their arms, and we drank the King's health in champagne, and fired a volley, the Princess's health in Burgundy, and fired a volley, and all the rest of the Royal Family in claret, and fired a volley. We drank the Governor's health and fired another volley."

Surprisingly, everyone arose at a reasonable hour next morning, and they started home. On their return to civilization, Spotswood presented each of his companions with a golden horseshoe—some studded with precious stones—as a memento of the trip. The men thereafter referred to themselves as "Knights of the Golden Horseshoe."

This lighthearted exploration was probably the first "recreational excursion" into an area that has become one of the Nation's most popular vacationlands. Today much of it is preserved as Shenandoah National Park; but long before it became a park it was the site of a famous resort.

George Freeman Pollock grew up in Washington, D. C., in the late 1800's with a love for the outdoors and the wildlife there. His attic rooms held a miniature museum and zoo, filled with stuffed animals and live owls, flying squirrels, fish, and a raccoon.

His father owned an interest in a 5,371-acre tract on the Blue Ridge mountain called Stony Man, property left from an abandoned copper mining venture, and young Pollock visited the mountain in 1886. He was overwhelmed. "Beauty beyond description!" he wrote. ". . . The wind blew hard and it was cold, but I did not feel it, and what a view! To say that I was carried away is putting it mildly. . . . I raved and shouted and probably would have yodelled if I had known, at that time, how to yodel."

Despite the relative inaccessibility of the region, disputes with squatters, and the prevalence of rattlesnakes, Pollock determined to build a resort camp on Stony Man—so named for its profile. In 1894 he issued his first circular inviting guests: "A feature of the camp life will be *large campfires every pleasant night. . . . Tramping parties will leave camp every pleasant day* with competent guides to visit the many points of interest. . . ."

Board was $7 a week, and a tent equipped with "cots, chairs, washstand, pitcher, lantern, bowl, etc." cost another $2.50.

As the popularity of the resort grew, gardens and a herd of cows supplemented the food bought from mountaineers, and the entertainment became more lavish: On one occasion guests saw a circus followed by a Wild West show in the afternoon, then spent the evening at a fancy-dress ball.

Pollock's business activities never superseded his interest in natural history. As a single example, he was fascinated by rattlesnakes and collected them for several zoos, paying $2 each for large, healthy specimens. Mountaineers would strip a long section of bark from a young chestnut tree and let the bark curl back to form a tube, into which went a captured snake. Damp moss plugged the ends.

He worked tirelessly for the establishment of Shenandoah National Park, whose melodious Indian name, says tradition, means "daughter of the stars." He was present on July 3, 1936, to hear President Franklin D. Roosevelt dedicate it "to the present and succeeding generations of Americans for the recreation and re-creation which we shall find here." When Pollock died in 1949, his ashes were scattered over the slopes of his beloved mountains. His Skyland resort continues in operation.

Long and narrow, Shenandoah extends for some 80 miles along Virginia's Blue Ridge, wearing the cloak of blue haze that gives the mountains their name. Skyline Drive traces the ridge crest, and the Appalachian Trail follows generally the same route.

The great majority of visitors to the park come simply to admire the views along Skyline, especially in fall when the turning leaves splash slopes and valleys with color. Others fish rushing trout streams, ride the bridle trails, camp at one of the four large, modern campgrounds — or hike.

One midsummer evening Jill, Dick, and I joined a group around a campfire at the amphitheater in Big Meadows Campground. We sang for a while; then, after the last refrain of "Clementine" had faded away, a vivacious ranger-naturalist named Aggie Crandall narrated a slide show. Her theme: Nature's beauty is all around us, in small things as well as large; a pattern of shadow on a leaf can be as breathtaking as a vast panorama.

Aggie's enthusiasm for the park was infectious, so the next day I rejoined her at the Big Meadows Visitor Center. I found her with two dozen visitors she was about to guide on a four-hour "explorers' hike." She

"Meals from improbable combinations, in improbable places..."

worried especially over the state of footwear, and before we set out sent one woman back to her car to put on socks under her sneakers.

When we reached a burned-over area, Aggie explained that a severe fire can sterilize the soil. "But in grassy areas like Big Meadows, a fire would sweep through quickly without damaging the soil. The Indians and the early settlers often used fire to clear an area."

A brownish-gray groundhog bounced along ahead of us. Aggie identified wild flowers and shrubs: "This is dogbane," she said, gently folding a leaf from a low, sparse shrub until it cracked slightly, and a drop of milky fluid oozed out. "It's said to be poisonous to dogs."

Yellow spikes of goldenrod attracted our admiration; columbines dangled scarlet and yellow blossoms. Aggie led us gingerly around a hill of Allegheny mound-builder ants to prevent its being disturbed by our steps.

As we left the road to move through the pathless forest, she had us count off to make sure no one had been left behind. We stopped beside a stream, and from Aggie's belt pouch came tart candy drops for everyone. Then, compass in hand, she led us home past clusters of white yarrow, with leaves almost fernlike; touch-me-nots, whose mature pods explode when disturbed; and the spectacular orange turbans of turk's-cap lilies.

Later I talked with Aggie about her job. It was obvious she enjoyed it; I asked whether anything about it bothered her.

"I guess I'm frustrated most by not being able to reach more of the people who come to the park," she answered. "I think I reached everyone on the hike, but there are so many more who never meet a true believer. It's a little like being a missionary. But when I get a little discouraged, I take my own advice to go for a walk, maybe up Old Rag. It does wonders for me."

OLD RAG is a favorite of many. The late Harry Flood Byrd, former Governor of Virginia and United States Senator, climbed it as often as he could. It's not an easy peak. The trail ascends 2,400 feet in three miles, much of it over great boulders. But a spectacular view awaits at the top: the continuing irregular wall of the Blue Ridge to the west, the tile-like mosaic of foothill farmlands to the east.

Stony Man, where George Pollock spent so many happy hours, is another favorite vantage, and the climb is much easier. Early one morning we trudged to the summit for a breakfast that included cold rice and chocolate—one of Jill's meals of improbable combinations eaten in improbable places. The usual morning mist hid the valley below, and the wind tried to hurl us off the cliff. Buffeted but fascinated, we watched as the clinging mist slowly yielded to the wind and sun.

The park contains about 390 miles of footpaths, including its section of the Appalachian Trail and numerous marked nature walks. I dropped 15 cents into a box at the start of the Swamp Nature Trail, just off the parking lot at the Big Meadows amphitheater, and took from the box a booklet describing what I would see along the way. Stopping periodically to read, I walked two miles through second-growth woodland once almost denuded by lumbering, fire, and disease. Grasses and plants had re-established themselves first, of course; then shrubs and small trees. Eventually the recovery will bring back a mature oak-hickory forest.

Patches of haircap moss, like that I'd seen on Georgia's Blood Mountain, grew along the trail. Settlers dried it and used it for pillows and upholstery. They also made good use of the bark of the chestnut oak, for it yielded tannin needed to convert hides into leather. Here and there I saw an eastern hemlock, its purplish-brown bark deeply furrowed. Hemlock was heavily lumbered for use on the decks of sailing ships.

Ghostly snags of chestnut trees recalled one of the greatest tragedies ever to strike American forests. The chestnut was once the most common tree in the Blue Ridge. Its great spreading branches blossomed with creamy white flowers in the summer, and dropped bushels of sweet nuts to the ground in autumn. To mankind the chestnut was one of nature's most useful plants: Its lumber was fashioned into furniture, its small branches and chips saved for pulp; its durability made it ideal for fence posts, utility poles, and railroad ties; its abundance made it cheap. On Pollock's first trip to Stony Man he met a mountaineer dragging down two ties to be sold for 10 cents apiece. A sizable leather tanning industry was largely dependent on tannin extracted from the chestnut's wood and bark. The nuts were a significant item of food, and roasted chestnuts and chestnut stuffing added zest to many a meal.

About the turn of the century, a fungus from the Far East—*Endothia parasitica*—entered North America, apparently at New York. Within 50 years it had all but eliminated the chestnut from the eastern forests, destroying a total of more than nine million acres of trees.

Spores of the lethal fungus attacked through wounds in the trees. The spores were spread by the wind, by birds and beasts, by insects and men. One scientist found 7,000 spores—each one capable of killing a tree—clinging to the feet of a single woodpecker.

Scientists have searched the Orient for a species of chestnut resistant to the blight; they have tramped the forests of America looking for a chestnut that had proved naturally immune. A tree with the quality of the old chestnut has not been found, but promising hybrids have been developed, and the research continues.

The victimized trees themselves still fight: From their stumps sprouts rise, sometimes reaching a height of several feet and producing a few nuts before the blight returns. Perhaps from such sprouts, botanists surmise, nature will one day produce her own blight-resistant strain.

One man who well remembers shaking chestnut limbs and gathering the fallen nuts is Gurd A. Cave, a storekeeper and minister in Shenandoah, Virginia. Mr. Cave grew up within what is now the national park and lived there until 1937. He and his wife operate a weathered roadside store barely ten feet square. They stock such household essentials as canned milk, soup, crackers, aspirin, and soap. Gurd finished serving soft drinks to a group of youngsters before pausing to reminisce.

"The price of chestnuts started at $10 a bushel and went down as the season went on," Gurd told us. "Whenever there was a big storm we'd go out and pick 'em up off the ground. Otherwise we'd climb the tree and shake the branches. Some mountain people chopped down whole trees just to get the nuts—but we never did that." Money came also from peeling bark and selling it to tanneries. "The longest I was ever away from home was for five weeks one time in Covington, peeling bark and preaching."

Gurd was born near Dark Hollow Falls in March 1884. Chester A. Arthur was President, and in faraway New York City electric lights were just being installed. He went as far as sixth grade at a school about a mile from home. "My mother was a good truant officer," he said.

"I got saved when I was 20, and God called me to preach about two years later. I used to walk 20 miles a day and preach twice. Up and down the mountain." Born a Methodist, Gurd is now a minister of the Inland Faith Mountain Mission.

As we talked, Gurd's wife Dorothy stood shyly at his side, her white hair gathered into a bun, her wire-frame glasses catching the sunlight streaming through the open door — the store's only source of illumination. They have been married 65 years.

"I was 22 and she was . . . 16 or 17? We lived about four miles apart, her over on Tanner's Ridge.

"We had 11 children. One winter — a bad one, the snow covered the house — we lost two of them in two days to diphtheria. One died on a Tuesday morning at 7; the other on Wednesday at 9. Buried 'em in the same grave. We lost two more; but we managed to raise five boys and two girls.

"About 375 families lived in what's now the park. Our nearest neighbor was a quarter mile away. We had a four-room house and an orchard with 75 fruit trees." But starting in 1935 the Government began acquiring the private property within the designated park boundaries. "We couldn't do nothing about it. We were just mountain people, never been to court, so it was take the money or nothing. I got $385 for our place, when the lawyers were through with it. They burned it down after we moved out. There may be a few bricks from the chimney up there still. I've never been back."

The Shenandoah's four campgrounds are as crowded as those in the Smokies, and we had to stand in line for a shower. Along with the bears that make noise all night with the lids of garbage cans, there are skunks that tiptoe around tentsites and trailers looking for unattended food supplies. Bedded down on the fringe of the Big Meadows campground, I heard a rustling at the tent flap. I turned quickly to find myself eyeball-to-eyeball with one of the handsome little black-and-white creatures. Apparently I surprised him as much as he startled me. We regarded each other cautiously, then he turned and moved off into the campground. I waited for cries of alarm, but all remained silent.

White-tailed deer have staged a comeback in the park recently, after having been almost eliminated from Virginia by early settlers with their dogs, guns, and love of venison. Fifteen were released in 1935 in the southern section of the park, an ideal habitat for them with its forest cover, brushy open fields, and abandoned orchards. Today deer are common in the park. Hunters scouting along the fringe in season — and passing automobiles — keep the herd in check, so there seems no danger that they will overpopulate the park. We saw many of them at Big Meadows, along Skyline Drive, and on the trail. Near our shelter one evening a doe stood and watched us with great luminous brown eyes, her tail wagging like a puppy's.

In nearly six months of roaming the Appalachians, we saw only one poisonous snake. It was a rattlesnake here in the Shenandoah, and it was dead. We learned that a hiker had killed it the day before with his walking stick, when he couldn't get his dog to come away. He had thus violated two of the park regulations — one protecting all wildlife, and another requiring a leash on pets.

Shelters in the Shenandoah, as in the Smokies, are well patronized in summer. I arrived one rainy afternoon at the Lewis Falls Shelter — a six-man lean-to — in the company of a retired Methodist minister and his two grandsons. Five young men, including a park trail maintenance employee, were already present. Soon there arrived a couple from Annapolis, with a friend from North Carolina. We made room for everyone as we sat out a ten-minute hailstorm about five o'clock, watching wide-eyed when lightning split a tree a hundred yards away. Then, as we were cooking supper, out of the gloom and drizzle marched 23 Boy Scouts from Virginia Beach.

There was nothing to do but squeeze up and ask them in. Pandemonium! Boy Scouts everywhere — in the bunks, under the bunks, under the table. They had had a long day, bypassing one shelter because it was full, and hiking an extra six miles to reach this one. Moreover, they had been drenched the night before, and a contingent that had taken wet clothes and sleeping bags to a coin laundry had not yet returned, so half the group had nothing dry to sleep in.

The troop leaders — wearing rather grim expressions at this point — extended the shelter by rigging an awning of large plastic sheets. It reached out over their fire — and funneled smoke into the shelter. Gathering around the fire, the Scouts tried to dry out. Steam rose from the boys and mixed with the smoke. Then the smoke took on still a different odor; a wet boot placed too near the heat began smoldering.

About 10:30 p.m., when all the boys had been fed and settled down, the word suddenly was passed that they were moving out. Someone had arranged to truck them to the next shelter up the trail, which was empty. So 23 Scouts arose, reassembled packs, and searched the dark shelter for lost articles. One had two left boots; but since no one would admit having two right ones, he limped away in them, last in line.

*T*O TRY TO PREVENT just such jam-ups, the park has established about 20 back-country campgrounds, unimproved sites away from roads and the heavily used sections of the park. Each is accessible only by trail and has a good source of water. There are no shelters or fireplaces but all have stone fire rings. The campgrounds will be moved periodically to allow the area to recover from heavy use.

It was en route to such a back-country campground that we encountered a dozen youngsters from Glaydin School and Camp near Leesburg, Virginia. Their young counselors — bearded Tony Novak and blond Lorrie Buchanan — dealt unperturbed with their boisterous charges as they helped them organize their packs at roadside where the school bus had let them off. One girl had brought a blanket and pillow, another an enormous jar of peanut butter. From one pack waved leafy stalks of celery.

"A few of these are kids who don't fit into regular camps for one reason or another," Tony told us. "It's really a mixed bag. Some of them have their camp fees paid by various social agencies; others' parents pay their way. Several go to school at Glaydin and stay on in the summer for camp."

In some circles Tony might be called a hippie, because of his long hair and beard, and I asked him how he liked working with little rebels. "It's hard for me to be authoritarian," he said. "I still think of *myself* as a rebel. And here I am trying to keep track of these kids. But I really enjoy it."

The wide assortment of packs finally got loaded and the little band took off down the trail that led about two miles to their campsite.

We found them there next morning, making toast over a fire struggling to recover from a dousing of cocoa. Seven-year-old Matthew, instructed to dispose of some leftover hot chocolate, had accidentally poured it on the fire.

No one had scolded him, and he soon had the fire blazing again. Matt was a good example of what the camp was trying to achieve. Frightened and whining when he arrived, he had begged to return to his mother and the maid at home in a Washington suburb. Now, after two weeks of adventure and some responsibility, he was becoming an exuberant extrovert. Originally scheduled for only three weeks of camp, he hoped to be allowed to remain for the final three. That afternoon Matt was the only one brave enough to slide down the foaming rocks of White Oak Falls into the pool where the others were swimming.

Our last morning in the Shenandoah, we got up before daylight and followed our dancing flashlight beams to Big Meadows. There we separated, each to be alone with the sunrise. I chose a slope at the meadow's edge, and settled down to watch the black world turn to gray.

"I'll tell you how the sun rose," wrote Emily Dickinson, "—a ribbon at a time." Bands of pink and violet appeared above the mountains to the east. Far above, a turkey buzzard circled, already in sunlight. Meadowlarks, catbirds, and juncos greeted the gathering light with a chorus of calls. Two deer crossed the meadow while another circled warily behind me.

Over a distant peak, finally, a pinpoint of fiery orange appeared. I looked down: For a few moments my chest was bright with sunlight while my knees were still in shadow.

When the sun was well up, we turned to another miracle: great beds of ripe blueberries. We picked until our fingers and lips were stained and our pockets were full. Then we recrossed the dew-soaked meadow to our camp, and ate them all for breakfast.

Tripod in hand, Dick crosses the "nose" of Stony Man in Shenandoah National Park. Lava extruded 800 million years ago was later metamorphosed into the dense greenstone that caps much of the Blue Ridge.

"I walked those mountains up and down, night and day. Spent all my best years up there, preaching and working."

With the park's establishment, Dorothy and Gurd

Cave left the mountains. Now he keeps store in the Shenandoah Valley — and goes on preaching.

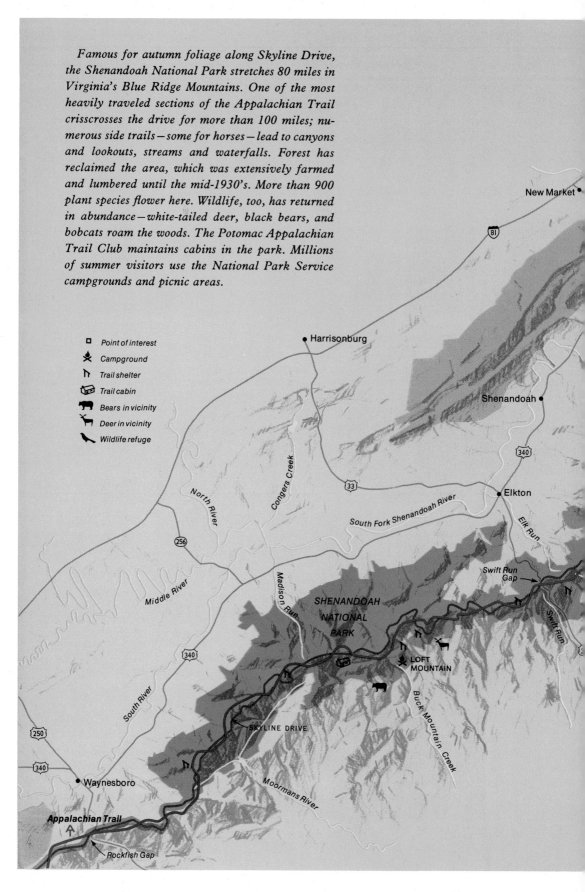

Famous for autumn foliage along Skyline Drive, the Shenandoah National Park stretches 80 miles in Virginia's Blue Ridge Mountains. One of the most heavily traveled sections of the Appalachian Trail crisscrosses the drive for more than 100 miles; numerous side trails—some for horses—lead to canyons and lookouts, streams and waterfalls. Forest has reclaimed the area, which was extensively farmed and lumbered until the mid-1930's. More than 900 plant species flower here. Wildlife, too, has returned in abundance—white-tailed deer, black bears, and bobcats roam the woods. The Potomac Appalachian Trail Club maintains cabins in the park. Millions of summer visitors use the National Park Service campgrounds and picnic areas.

□   Point of interest

Campground

Trail shelter

Trail cabin

Bears in vicinity

Deer in vicinity

Wildlife refuge

New Market

Harrisonburg

Shenandoah

Elkton

North River

Congers Creek

Middle River

Madison Run

South Fork Shenandoah River

Elk Run

Swift Run Gap

Swift Run

SHENANDOAH NATIONAL PARK

LOFT MOUNTAIN

Buck Mountain Creek

South River

SKYLINE DRIVE

Waynesboro

Moormans River

Appalachian Trail

Rockfish Gap

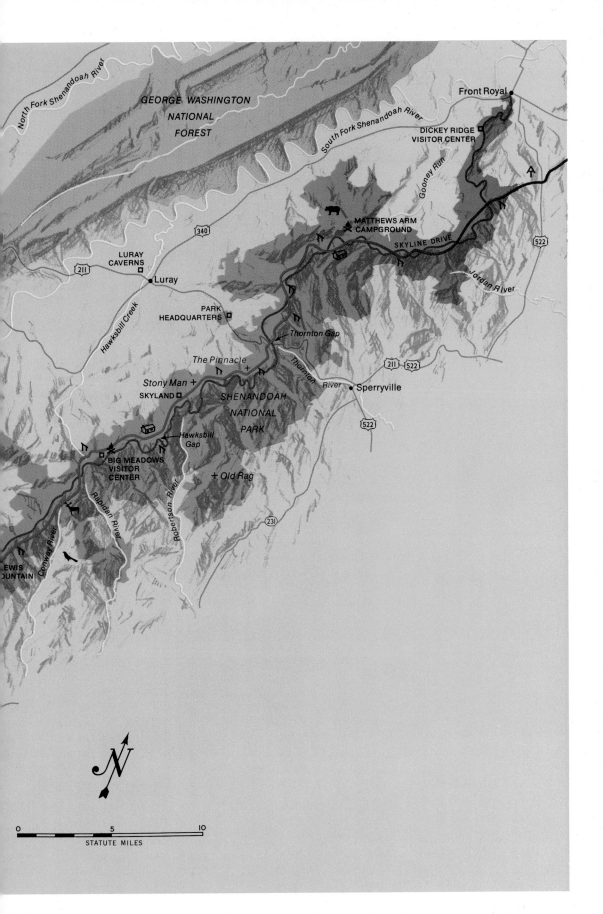

North Fork Shenandoah River

GEORGE WASHINGTON
NATIONAL
FOREST

Front Royal

South Fork Shenandoah River

DICKEY RIDGE
VISITOR CENTER

Gooney Run

340

LURAY
CAVERNS

211   Luray

MATTHEWS ARM
CAMPGROUND

SKYLINE DRIVE

Jordan River

522

PARK
HEADQUARTERS

Hawksbill Creek

Thornton Gap

The Pinnacle

Stony Man

SKYLAND

SHENANDOAH
NATIONAL
PARK

Thornton River

211   522

Sperryville

522

Hawksbill
Gap

Old Rag

BIG MEADOWS
VISITOR
CENTER

Robertson River

231

Rapidan River

Conway River

LEWIS
MOUNTAIN

N

0   5   10
STATUTE MILES

Incandescent clusters of goldenrod gone to seed glow in Big Meadows, 3,500 feet high in the Blue Ridge. At left, protected by laws that prohibit all hunting within Shenandoah National Park, a white-tailed doe in summer coat enters the meadows. Morning moisture beads a fragile five-starred columbine.

On a two-day expedition to the park, young campers stop beside White Oak Falls, reached by a side trail. While 13-year-old Denise Calhoun daydreams on a log across a stream, 10-year-olds Mary Ann Shore (left) and Cheryl McBride rinse their dishes in a still pool.

Bizarre, often beautiful plant life thrives on the damp forest floor. The fungus Hydnellum (top left) digests organic material in the rich soil. The bracket fungus (Fomes) at center left lives on a tree. Coprinus mushrooms, or inky caps (bottom left), exhibit the phenomenon of auto-digestion: When mature, they secrete an enzyme that dissolves their own tissues, reducing the plant to an inky black liquid. Rainwater sits in Tricholomopsis fungus growing from a rotten log. The appearance of the parasitic herb Monotropa earned for it the common name Indian pipe (lower right). Soft, warty scales cover a poisonous Amanita.

5.

Across
Mason-Dixon
to the Delaware

"**T**UESDAY 3. Ready to march at 7. Took the Canal Boats. Stoped at Point of Rocks 1 hour & landed Harper's Fery about 11 o.c. Bivouaced in a grove close by. Had to keep very still & light no matches, as a rebel Battery was on the opposite side river." In September of 1861, Jill's great-grandfather Charles N. Richards described in his diary his visit to Harpers Ferry as a Union soldier in the Civil War.

Almost exactly 110 years later we perched on Chimney Rock, an outcrop on the bluffs south of the West Virginia town, and watched the Shenandoah and Potomac Rivers angle through the Blue Ridge and merge.

"Wednesday 4. Went a ¼ mile down, saw a house riddled with Balls, fired by the Rebs in a rifled cannon. While standing on the embankment of the N. Y. Tammany Reg. a Ball came within arm's length of me. I kept under cover then."

If Charles climbed to the heights from which we caught our first glimpse of the town, he didn't record it. From there Harpers Ferry looks as if it had been flung against the side of the hill, it clings so precariously; a good shake, one suspects, would send the whole town sliding into the river.

Water power to turn machinery — the force of the river rushing through the narrow gorge — determined the town's location. In 1796 Congress established a gun factory here, and other industry followed; on Virginius Island rose a sawmill, flour mill, cotton textile plant, iron foundry, carriage factory, and a row of dwellings. An intricate system of underground culverts carried water from the river to power the mills. By the 1840's a railroad cut westward to the coalfields.

But history laid a heavy hand on Harpers Ferry.

At dusk on Chimney Rock, high above the Potomac and Shenandoah Rivers, Jill softly plays her recorder. Across the Shenandoah lights blink on in Harpers Ferry, where her great-grandfather fought during the Civil War.

Its most famous visitor—abolitionist John Brown, from Kansas— arrived one rainy night in October 1859. With a small band of followers he hoped to capture the U. S. Arsenal and use the weapons to equip an uprising of slaves in the South. But after the town's initial fright, citizens and militiamen surrounded the raiders in the armory firehouse, where Col. Robert E. Lee led 90 Marines in an assault that killed or wounded most of Brown's men and took their leader prisoner. He was tried for murder, fomenting a slave insurrection, and treason against Virginia, and hanged in Charles Town in December.

When war broke out in April 1861, retreating Union soldiers burned the arsenal and armory to keep them from Confederate hands. A couple of months later Southern soldiers destroyed the railroad bridge across the Potomac. The bridge made the town a strategic prize; the surrounding heights made it, as one Yankee said, "no more defensible than a well bottom." Nine times Rebels burned the span, nine times Northern engineers repaired it. In September 1862, when General Lee was invading Maryland with high hopes for Confederate independence, he sent Stonewall Jackson against this key point. Jackson's columns occupied the surrounding heights and began shelling Union positions; soon he had 12,000 prisoners. Such episodes left the town a wreck.

Later in the century floods all but swept the community away. It has never recovered, economically, from the loss of its industry to the batterings of war and nature.

From 1936 to 1948, the Appalachian Trail passed through Harpers Ferry, and hikers were ferried across the Shenandoah in punts. Today they cross the Potomac on a highway bridge about a mile downstream, but the National Park Service plans to build a footbridge on the pilings of the old railroad span.

The Chesapeake and Ohio Canal, now designated a national historical park, passes near Harpers Ferry on its way between Cumberland, Maryland, and the District of Columbia. Begun in 1828, the canal operated as a commercial waterway—bypassing the falls and rapids of the Potomac— until 1924, when a flood damaged many of its locks. Its 185-mile towpath is a favorite route for hikers and bicyclists.

HIKERS in northern Virginia walk in the footsteps of a famous surveyor. All the lands between the Potomac and Rappahanock Rivers were granted to the Fairfax family by Charles II. In 1748, when Thomas, Lord Fairfax was looking for a manor site, he sent his brother George William Fairfax and a promising 16-year-old youth named George Washington to survey a 120,000-acre tract. They followed the route of today's U. S. Highway 50 across the Blue Ridge, passed through Ashby Gap, and pursued the Potomac upstream through the Alleghenies. Turning south, they returned to the Shenandoah Valley and recrossed the mountains at Snickers Gap—today's Virginia Highway 7.

Most of the distance—260 trail miles—between Harpers Ferry and the Delaware Water Gap to the northeast is taken up by two mountain masses, called South Mountain and Blue Mountain, separated by the Susquehanna River. Early travelers on South Mountain may have included fugitive slaves making their way northward along the Underground Railroad. Five of John Brown's men used the same route to escape after the raid on Harpers Ferry failed.

In 1794, three years after Congress began taxing whiskey, South Mountain nearly spawned an armed rebellion. Almost every spring of water on the mountain had its still, and the angry owners gathered to march in protest on the tax collectors at Frederick, Maryland. But they had second thoughts and turned back when they learned that federal troops were waiting for them.

Home distilling continued in the region, however, and became so firmly established that during the Prohibition era of the 20th century it occurred to a man named Spencer Weaver that he might organize the moonshiners into a highly profitable syndicate. He offered steady wages plus bonuses and fringe benefits; if jailed, a member continued to receive his pay and was loaned money to re-establish his still when he got out. Weaver even had an informal contract with a funeral home in Harpers Ferry covering burial costs of slain members, and he paid their widows a pension.

The official guidebook to the Maryland section of the trail concludes the story: "But prosperity may have ruined Weaver; he started drinking his own product and mild heart attacks followed. One night he backed his auto into the C&O Canal and was found dead."

It is difficult to realize, in an age of rapid and comfortable transcontinental travel, what a formidable barrier the Appalachian Mountains represented in the period of exploration and settlement. Pathfinders looked for gaps in the mountains, passages through which soldiers and settlers could follow. Now highways run through the gaps, and the trail descends—usually steeply—to cross them, then climbs again on the other side.

Since the gaps became funnels where traffic concentrated, inns and taverns were often located there. One of these, South Mountain Inn in Turners Gap, is still operating, within shouting distance of the trail.

There was only a foot and bridle path through the gap until 1755, when Maj. Gen. Edward Braddock's army built a road. It was later designated part of the National Road, which ran from Cumberland, Maryland, westward to Vandalia, Illinois. Right on the heels of Braddock's roadbuilders came Robert Turner, who built his inn in 1759. Travelers could spend the night, get their horses reshod, or exchange tired mounts for fresh.

In the next two centuries many famous Americans slept here, including at least half a dozen who held or were to hold the office of President: Jackson, Van Buren, Harrison, Tyler, Polk, Lincoln. Tradition says Daniel Webster and Henry Clay spent many an hour in conversation and debate before the fireplace.

War, piety, and peace have set their stamp on the property. In 1876 a widow bought it for a summer home. Disturbed by the sinfulness of the people of the area, she built a stone chapel that overlooks the trail. In the 1920's the Sisters of the Holy Cross came here on summer retreats.

But South Mountain Inn served as a Confederate command post on one of the most dramatic days of the Civil War: September 14, 1862. Lee had divided his army, sending Jackson to Harpers Ferry—and the Union commander George McClellan knew it, from lost Confederate orders. Here was the opportunity to cross the Blue Ridge at several gaps and destroy the enemy piecemeal; he would never get a better chance. But along the crest that would later become the Appalachian Trail, the Rebel rear guard dug in their heels: at Turners Gap, at Fox Gap, at Crampton. On South Mountain they fought a delaying action that permitted Lee to reunite his men and take a strong position to the west.

We followed them, making a short detour to the Antietam National Battlefield Site, where Jill's great-grandfather was nearly killed when a bullet smashed his nose, cheek, and upper jaw. But he survived, and returned home. Many did not.

Lee had disposed his outnumbered units on high ground before the little town of Sharpsburg when McClellan's forces attacked on September 17. Fighting that rose to frenzy lasted from dawn until late afternoon, and caused more casualties—about 22,500—than any other day of the war.

The battle amounted to a draw, but Lee slipped away to Virginia on the night of the 18th, so the North had at least the appearance of a victory. It was an opportunity President Lincoln had been waiting for: With the Southern offensive checked, he announced his Emancipation Proclamation effective January 1, 1863, freeing the slaves in all areas under Confederate control. The proclamation ended the possibility that Great Britain and France would recognize Confederate independence—for no European power would support the cause of slavery against a Union dedicated to human freedom.

Today the stilled cannons point empty muzzles toward a quiet horizon. Well-tended roads carry visitors past signs explaining the action and monuments commemorating soldiers of both sides. As we stood on a shoulder of Bloody Lane—the sunken road where some 3,000 were killed or wounded—heat waves shimmered across the green hills. Several crows circled overhead. Only the crickets chirping in the grass broke the silence.

WE STEPPED from Maryland into Pennsylvania across one of the Nation's most historic boundaries: the Mason-Dixon line. In the 1760's two British surveyors, Charles Mason and Jeremiah Dixon, were commissioned to survey the long-disputed boundary dividing the colonies of Pennsylvania and Maryland. As it turned out, the Mason-Dixon line also became the geographical division between the so-called southern and northern states—although when the great rupture of civil war came, Maryland remained loyal to the Union.

When the line was surveyed, limestone markers—imported for some reason from England, although there is native limestone nearby—were placed at intervals. The marker for mile 91 is a short distance from the point where the trail crosses the boundary.

Only a few miles into Pennsylvania the hiker comes on the first evidence of the state's early charcoal-iron industry. The trail passes among the picnic tables of Caledonia State Park in the 80,000-acre Michaux State Forest. The park preserves the site of the Caledonia Ironworks, once the property of abolitionist lawyer Thaddeus Stevens. The ironworks was destroyed during the Gettysburg campaign in 1863.

Pennsylvania's large deposits of iron ore, its broad forests ready to be converted into charcoal, and its streams so easily harnessed for waterpower made it the young Nation's leading producer of iron. Just before the Civil War the state supplied more than half of America's raw iron. Pittsburgh had 30 large foundries and numerous smaller ones, turning out steam engines, railroad equipment, and heavy machinery to meet the continuing demands of the industrial revolution.

Throughout these woods the remains of old charcoal hearths can still be seen—round, level clearings where trees have not yet re-established themselves. About 1840 anthracite coal replaced charcoal in iron manufacture. Until then, workers made the charcoal by stacking logs, covering them with moist earth, and setting them afire to smolder for about ten days.

Near Caledonia the trail passes an old Civilian Conservation Corps camp that later housed prisoners of war interned from German submarines captured during World War II.

A few miles farther up the trail is the Pine Grove Furnace. Its owners had an interest in the Cumberland Valley Railroad, and to boost profits they decided to venture into the resort business. In the vicinity of their ironworks they built a park and a lake, and constructed rustic lodges. In summer, groups for business meetings and Sunday school picnics sometimes arrived from Philadelphia at the rate of ten coachloads a day.

Just north of Dillsburg, Pennsylvania, South Mountain finally slopes off to level ground like an exhausted giant sinking to rest, and for about 13 miles the trail runs across the Cumberland Valley on dusty roads lined with prosperous farms. It was this productive region that General Lee coveted as a source of subsistence for his army, until he was turned back at Antietam and finally at Gettysburg.

At Yellow Breeches Creek, James and Nellie Brymesser and their three sons keep a herd of 150 Holstein dairy cows on 700 acres adjacent to the trail. We walked up the driveway of the large brick house, and in the rear found the washing out on the line, chickens clucking in their coops, and Mrs. Brymesser hosing down the back porch.

The Brymessers come close to being self-sufficient. In addition to the milk production, there are eggs from 800 chickens; the men butcher 20 hogs a year; and Nellie raises a garden. "I once froze seven bushels of green beans," she told us, "and I used to make 100 pounds of butter at a time and put it in the freezer. When the boys were growing up I canned 300 quarts of tomato juice a year." We could see green clumps of rhubarb growing beside the garage; golden chrysanthemums were blooming in the flower beds.

The Brymessers were married in 1936, and began their life together on an 80-acre farm with seven cows. They lost them all to an epidemic about five years later. Four years after that, Bang's disease killed another 26.

"Since then," said James, who had joined us on the porch, "we vaccinate everything. Haven't lost a cow since—nor had to buy one."

Soon the three sons—Stanley, Steve, and Sheldon, husky young men tanned by years in the sun—reassembled from their midmorning naps. We understood the nap custom when we learned that they rise at 3:30 a.m. to do the milking—every day of the year, holiday or not, rain or shine.

"We get about 600 gallons of milk a day," James told us, standing in the shade of a huge oak tree in the front yard. "A tank truck picks it up every other day and hauls it to Philadelphia.

"We have 280 acres in corn, 54 in wheat, and 65 in barley—all for feed for the cows—but we still have to buy some corn."

He stood surveying his realm. Corn higher than our heads was turning golden in the late summer sun. Across the road, cows stood munching and lowing contentedly in the barnyard. Nearby, baby pigs squealed and chased each others' curly tails.

"I've been doing a man's work since I was nine," James said. "I was driving a four-horse team when I was 15. It's been a hard life but a good one. You can see things happen on a farm—the results of your labors are right there in front of you."

From the Brymesser place the trail continues across Cumberland Valley. At the intersection of Old Stone House Road and Pennsylvania Highway 641, we found a welcome surprise for hikers: a roadside produce market set up on a low, three-sided wagon. Nevin Shellenberger sells vegetables from a nearby farm: firm roasting ears of corn, yellow onions, plump red tomatoes, acorn squash, dark green cucumbers. "Hikers come by once in a while," he said, with a slight German accent. "I give them a couple tomatoes—ripe one for today, another not so ripe for tomorrow. They all ask about water and I show them the spigot over there," he said, pointing across the road.

A tall, rangy man with an angular and expressive face, Mr. Shellenberger also sells brooms that he makes himself in the slow periods between customers. "The handles come from South America," he said, "but I grow my own broom-corn for the brushes." He demonstrated how he makes them, chopping off excess stalk and binding it to the handle. "I can make about three an hour if I push it," he said. "I sell them at craft fairs as well as here at the stand."

As we left, he pressed on us half a dozen ears of sweet white corn. That night, having wrapped them in foil and roasted them in glowing coals, we ate them piping hot for supper.

AFTER WALKING under the hurtling traffic of the Pennsylvania Turnpike and across a bridge over the shallow, rock-strewn waters of the wide Susquehanna River, we found ourselves in St. Anthony's Wilderness, an uninhabited forest administered by the Pennsylvania Game Commission. The woods around us were quiet, but from the nearby Indiantown Gap Military Reservation came the repetitive chatter of machine gun fire.

The forest was filled with fading reminders of vanished Americans. For several miles the trail followed an old stagecoach road, now a grassy, narrow track that wound around the hills. Boulders the size of basketballs were partially embedded in the road; they must have made the stage ride a memorable one.

Soon we came to a junction important to horseback riders: Here ends the Horse-Shoe Trail, a 120-mile blazed route that begins at Valley Forge. A series of hostels extends along it.

All that remained of the old coal-mining town of Yellow Springs Village were several foundations and some crumbled stone walls. We wandered through the ruins into a backyard where juncos hopped undisturbed from stone to stone.

Old coal mines abound in this section, the slopes of their bomb-crater pits now covered with grass. We crossed the abandoned right-of-way of a branch of the Philadelphia and Reading Railroad, cinders crunching beneath our feet though the rails and ties were long gone. The August sun filtered through swaying hemlocks, and fragmented shadows moved along before us.

Of the ghost settlement of Rausch Gap, nothing remained except ruined foundations, a dry stone-lined well half full of dead leaves, and a sign nailed to a tree:

Community Well
Used by Populace of Rausch Gap
1850-1900
Erected by Pine Grove Boy Scouts

Back on gravel roads, we stopped at a farmhouse to ask directions, and the accent of the blond woman who greeted us was an instant reminder that we were in Pennsylvania Dutch country.

These Pennsylvanians are "German Dutch" (*Deutsch*), not "Holland Dutch." They are the descendants of German immigrants who pushed out from the Philadelphia area in the early 18th century.

They sprinkled the map with such whimsical place names as Mascot, Hinkletown, Bird in Hand, and Paradise. They built neat, sturdy houses, worked hard on their farms, painted their barns with hex signs, and gradually divorced themselves from the march of contemporary society, preferring older ways.

Every year their craftsmen gather in Hershey — a town that often smells tantalizingly of bubbling chocolate — to demonstrate skills and sell handicrafts. We arrived on opening day of the Pennsylvania Dutch Days celebration and found the Hershey Sports Arena jammed with people. Several thousand visitors milled among booths and tables where artists and craftsmen displayed their work.

Half a dozen women of the Palmyra Church of the Brethren sat around a square frame, painstakingly stitching a quilt. Each Wednesday they gather in the church basement to work on quilts, and they have been coming to the Dutch Days event every year since it began in 1949. The year before our visit they had made $2,500 for their church.

We watched a weaver, a cigar maker, a candle dipper, a barn sign painter, a glass blower. Mrs. Earl R. Horst of Lebanon, an expert at rug hooking, had made 116 colorful rugs, 20 chair seats, and 75 hot pads since the previous October.

Edward Campbell of Boiling Springs played one of the violins he had made, explaining that at least 400 hours of work go into each of his instruments. He uses only wood from the Alps — spruce for the top, maple for the sides and back. "Above a certain altitude in the mountains," he said, "the seasons don't vary much, so the grain is even. Uneven grain is bad for a violin's tone."

I asked what started him on a career as a violin maker. "I had a fiddle that needed fixing when I was a little boy," he said. "So I fixed it. I've been making violins ever since. I'm working on number 136 now."

Outside at the "Farmarama," Noah's Menagerie drew squeals from children attracted by a mother hen and chicks, a duck and ducklings, a mare and her foal, a dog and her puppies, and a couple of cows that, it appeared, would surely soon become mothers. An old steam engine chugged dutifully as it drove a threshing and baling machine. Swab's Dutch Band strolled and tooted among the crowd. At the food tent we followed barbecued chicken with shoofly pie, rich with molasses and spices.

Back on the trail, we crossed the path of some infamous 18th-century hikers who contributed to the friction that brought on the French and Indian War. In 1737, with English settlers advancing into Delaware Indian country and the Delawares grudgingly giving ground, a novel agreement was reached: The Indians would let white men inhabit the land along the Delaware River as far upstream as a man could walk in a day and a half. The Indians had in mind a normal pace; the whites did not. Thomas Penn, descendant of the founder of Pennsylvania, selected three young athletes, had them secretly reconnoiter a trail, and promised £5 and 500 acres to the man who walked the farthest. Edward Marshall covered more than 65 miles in the allotted time—about twice the distance the Delawares had anticipated. They never forgot nor forgave the Englishmen's stratagem.

The Delaware River has cut through the Appalachians near Stroudsburg, Pennsylvania, to create the Delaware Water Gap—a spectacular, two-mile-long gorge, its humps forested, its sheer face barren. From the Mount Minsi fire tower we got a commanding view of the mountain range, cleft by the river as though cosmic earthmovers had gouged the channel. Here the trail drops more than a thousand feet to the banks where the Delaware flows undeterred on its way to the sea.

Young fairgoers tumble in a stack of straw piled up for just such roughhousing during Pennsylvania Dutch Days at Hershey.

To the accompaniment of a kirtan, a spiritual chant in preparation for meditation, aspirants of Ananda Marga (the Path of Bliss) offer fruit to the Supreme Being as an act of devotion. The offering concludes a three-day retreat near Pine Grove. For other residents of rural southern Pennsylvania, weekends bring more-familiar pleasures: Sweethearts stroll a quiet country road; a backyard picnic brings together three generations of two families.

"When we chant
the kirtan,
we merge into
one spirit."

Too rocky for profitable farming and a barrier to trade, the high ridge country north of Shenandoah National Park carries the Appalachian Trail past, rather than through, history. The footpath skirts Harpers Ferry, where restored buildings and a museum commemorate the Civil War period—and where stand cliffs Thomas Jefferson called "monuments of a war between rivers and mountains." After climbing South Mountain in Maryland and southern Pennsylvania, the trail crosses rich farmlands in the Cumberland Valley; lack of shade on this level stretch can make summer tramping uncomfortable. North of the Susquehanna River, more than 75 species of wildlife find haven on state game lands. The trail hugs the crest of Blue Mountain, where occasional outcrops offer broad views of the valleys.

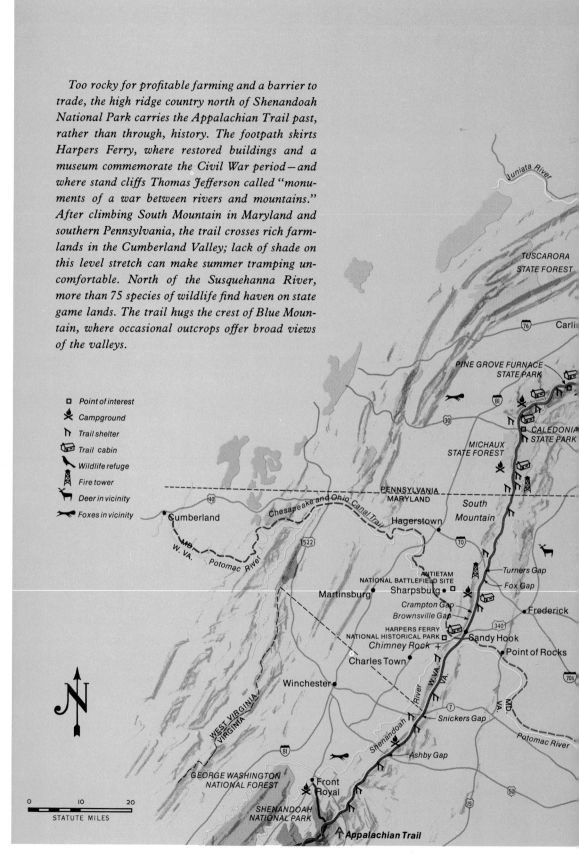

Point of interest

Campground

Trail shelter

Trail cabin

Wildlife refuge

Fire tower

Deer in vicinity

Foxes in vicinity

TUSCARORA STATE FOREST

Juniata River

Carlisle

PINE GROVE FURNACE STATE PARK

CALEDONIA STATE PARK

MICHAUX STATE FOREST

PENNSYLVANIA
MARYLAND

Cumberland

Chesapeake and Ohio Canal Trail

Hagerstown

South Mountain

Potomac River

Martinsburg

Sharpsburg

ANTIETAM NATIONAL BATTLEFIELD SITE

Turners Gap

Fox Gap

Crampton Gap

Brownsville Gap

Frederick

HARPERS FERRY NATIONAL HISTORICAL PARK

Chimney Rock

Charles Town

Sandy Hook

Point of Rocks

Winchester

Shenandoah River

Snickers Gap

Potomac River

WEST VIRGINIA
VIRGINIA

GEORGE WASHINGTON NATIONAL FOREST

Front Royal

SHENANDOAH NATIONAL PARK

Ashby Gap

Appalachian Trail

N

0   10   20
STATUTE MILES

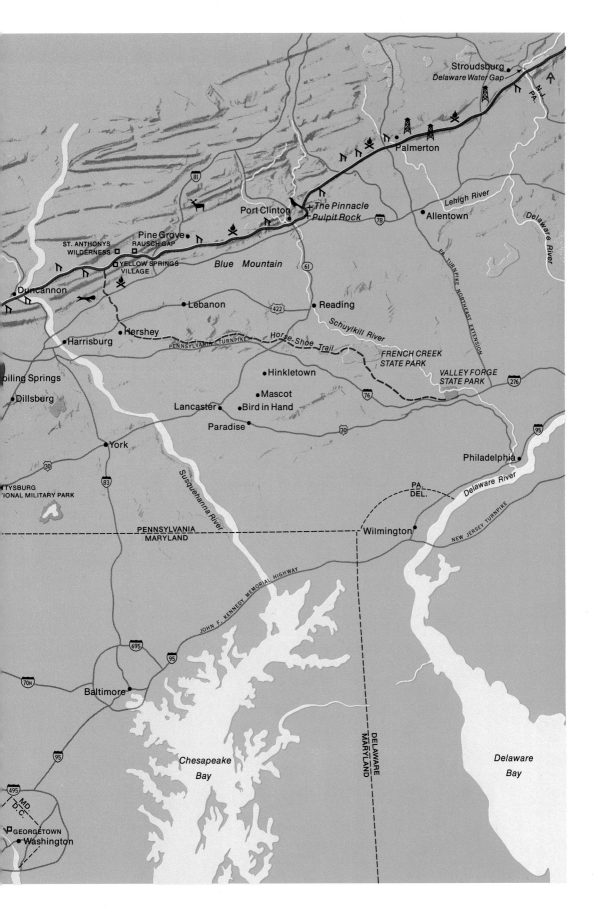

Stroudsburg
Delaware Water Gap

PA.
N.J.

Palmerton

Lehigh River

Delaware River

The Pinnacle
Pulpit Rock
Port Clinton

Allentown

81

78

Pine Grove

ST. ANTHONYS
WILDERNESS
RAUSCH GAP

YELLOW SPRINGS
VILLAGE

Blue Mountain

61

PA. TURNPIKE NORTHEAST EXTENSION

Duncannon

Lebanon

422

Reading

Schuylkill River

Horse-Shoe Trail

FRENCH CREEK
STATE PARK

Harrisburg

Hershey

PENNSYLVANIA TURNPIKE

VALLEY FORGE
STATE PARK

276

Hinkletown

76

oiling Springs

Mascot

Lancaster Bird in Hand

Dillsburg

Paradise

30

Philadelphia

York

30

83

Susquehanna River

PA.
DEL.

Delaware River

TYSBURG
IONAL MILITARY PARK

PENNSYLVANIA
MARYLAND

Wilmington

95

NEW JERSEY TURNPIKE

70N

695

95

JOHN F. KENNEDY MEMORIAL HIGHWAY

Baltimore

70N

DELAWARE
MARYLAND

495

MD.
D.C.

*Chesapeake
Bay*

*Delaware
Bay*

GEORGETOWN
Washington

"We get up at four to milk the cows, then feed a few hogs, and back to the barn..."

Ripening corn reaches golden tassels toward mare's-tail clouds — signs of changing weather — near Churchtown, Pennsylvania. Nearby, the trail crosses Yellow Breeches Creek at one corner of the farm of James Brymesser (above, center). He and his three sons, Steve (left), Stanley (right), and Sheldon, farm 700 acres, sharing the toil and the rewards. "There isn't too many families can work together this way," declared James Brymesser with pride.

High above traffic, Ron and Jill return a friendly wave from a motorist. The

concrete footbridge spans Interstate Highway 70 near Hagerstown, Maryland.

Gnarled skeletons of trees, some destroyed by industrial contamination and others by fire, overlook the smokestacks of the New Jersey Zinc Company's east plant in Palmerton, Pennsylvania. Farther south, a motorcyclist pauses on a wide, rock-strewn section of the trail. Although Congress in 1968 prohibited public use of motor vehicles on the Appalachian Trail, its isolation tempts owners of off-road vehicles. "We knew motorcycles scared away wildlife, damaged trailside vegetation, and dug ruts into the trail," said Jill, "but the most annoying thing was the ear-splitting noise, which carried far into the woods." Near Duncannon, painted names and initials deface Hawk Rock. "But we saw surprisingly little vandalism along the trail," Ron reported. "Its excellent condition proves that most hikers heed the backpackers' maxim, 'Take nothing but pictures; leave nothing but footprints.'"

6.

Land of
the Hudson
and Housatonic

LIKE DONKEYS in pursuit of dangling carrots—Jill objected to the comparison—we followed the neat white blazes that mark the Appalachian Trail, and crossed the Delaware into New Jersey. Platoons of volunteers wielding paint brushes and pruning shears have clearly defined the trail, no matter how thick or sparse the vegetation. Except for part of New Hampshire, where special cairns are in use, the volunteer crews have marked the trail by painting two-by-six-inch white blazes at intervals on trees, rocks, telephone poles, and fence posts. They use a paint made especially for the Appalachian Trail Conference: durable, slightly luminous, harmless to plants. The blazes need renewing about every two years.

It had long since become habit with us to look for these marks of reassurance that we had not strayed from the route.

The volunteers also clear weeds and brush from the sides of the trail, chop or saw and remove fallen trees and branches, and trim overhanging limbs to permit easy passage.

We were approaching our closest brush with megalopolis; New York City was barely 50 miles away, just over the horizon. Our expectations were not high for our walk through New Jersey and New York, and we wondered how the trail would negotiate what we envisioned as a solid concentration of shopping centers, superhighways, industrial plants, and housing developments.

We were pleasantly surprised. The view from the trail was quite the reverse of what we had anticipated: Instead of smokestacks, we saw low hills with cultivated fields rolling down their slopes; instead of look-alike subdivisions, quiet little towns set in narrow valleys, with courthouses

Only pedestrian toll booth on the Appalachian Trail charges each hiker a dime to cross the Hudson River on Bear Mountain Bridge in New York.

centered in green parks; instead of dams and reservoirs, small placid ponds where ducks trailed pennant-shaped wakes. The air was as clean as in the mountains to the south, and the people as friendly.

We hiked up to Sunfish Pond, a glacier-gouged, stream-fed hollow in the Kittatinny Mountains. The peaceful setting belied the controversy that had centered on the pond. A utility company wanted to use it as a reservoir for a hydroelectric generating plant; conservationists organized much-publicized opposition that, a few months after our visit, was successful.

Halfway up the hill to the pond, we passed a couple of neophyte hikers, two teen-age girls carrying part of their gear in a suitcase and the rest slung over their shoulders. Just off the trail a 20-foot chestnut sprout, the tallest we saw all summer, stretched several branches skyward.

We camped in a small clearing on the pond's shrubby bank. A glistening green frog sat on a rock and watched us make supper. As the stars appeared, he and his friends began a solemn chorus, and waves of their music lapped ashore all night.

Enormous bushes of swamp blueberries made breakfast easy. More than 20 species of blueberries grow east of the Great Plains, from above the Arctic Circle to Florida. They range in size and form from the ankle-high beds of the Shenandoah to these great bushes, which tower 15 feet.

CROSSING into New York, we soon came to the first section of the Appalachian Trail to be completed—a six-mile stretch finished in October 1923 in the Palisades Interstate Park, which now encompasses more than 75,000 acres. We crossed Beechy Bottom, the valley down which Brig. Gen. "Mad Anthony" Wayne led his soldiers in July 1779 on their way to Stony Point. Then, as we neared the Hudson, urban civilization caught up with us.

Descending steeply from the summit of Bear Mountain, we suddenly found ourselves on a paved sidewalk between a roller-skating rink and a grassy ski jump. Bear Mountain resort throbbed to the organ waltzes of the rink and the shouting of a dozen softball games. Swarms of people strolled, picnicked, and sprawled on the vast lawn beside Bear Mountain Inn. Workmen, preparing for the upcoming Labor Day weekend, were busy laying a floor for a huge banquet tent.

Beyond the inn we passed through a tunnel under U. S. Highway 9w and came to a large swimming pool and bathhouse. Dripping youngsters darted past, a few colliding with us when we were slow to sidestep.

With relief we left the crowds and entered the Nature Trail and Trailside Museum. The noise of the swimming pool faded as the path led us downward past fenced deer and caged foxes and raccoons. We could hear birds again, and feel the refreshing coolness of shade cast by towering hardwoods. Beside a tall bronze statue of Walt Whitman, I saw lines from his "Song of the Open Road" chiseled on a rock:

Afoot and light-hearted I take to the open road,
Healthy, free, the world before me,
The long brown path before me leading wherever I choose....

At the bear den, where a sleeping pair snored right through our visit, we came to the lowest point on the Appalachian Trail: 115.4 feet above sea level. We passed the site of old Fort Clinton—stormed and captured by the British during the Revolution and now a historical museum—and other museums devoted to nature study and geology.

Finally we reached Bear Mountain Bridge, paid the ten-cent toll for pedestrians, and crossed the Hudson River.

In 1609 Henry Hudson, an English navigator engaged by the Dutch East India Company to find a northwest passage to China, became the first European to sail up this river. Washington Irving's whimsical *Knickerbocker's History of New York* described Hudson as "a short, square, brawny old gentleman, with a double chin, a mastiff mouth, and a broad copper nose, which was supposed in those days to have acquired its fiery hue from the constant neighborhood of his tobacco-pipe. . . . He was remarkable for always jerking up his breeches when he gave out his orders, and his voice sounded not unlike the prattling of a tin trumpet."

Hudson and his men discovered Manhattan Island, skirmished with some Indians, and bought oysters from others. They made valuable explorations farther upstream as well, although Irving made light of their deductions: "After sailing, however, above a hundred miles up the river, he found the watery world around him begin to grow more shallow and confined, the current more rapid, and perfectly fresh—phenomena not uncommon in the ascent of rivers, but which puzzled the honest Dutchmen prodigiously. A consultation was therefore called, and having deliberated full six hours, they were brought to a determination by the ship's running aground—whereupon they unanimously concluded that there was but little chance of getting to China in this direction."

Hudson made one more search for a northern passage, this time sailing under the English flag, and probed the shores of Hudson Bay. But mutineers abandoned him, his young son, and part of the crew, and the deserted group was never found.

Where the trail crosses the Hudson River it is easy to see why it invited the famed navigator's exploration, for even here, 44 miles upstream from New York City, it is still an arm of the sea; its waters are brackish, and rise and fall with the ocean tides. The tidal action, in fact, extends as far north as Troy, about 150 miles from Lower New York Bay. The Mahican Indians called the river Muhheakunnuk, "great waters constantly in motion."

The Revolutionary War moved up and down the Hudson with the maneuvers of British warships. Because of the river's strategic location the British hoped to control it and thus cut the rebellious colonies in two. At West Point, at a sharp turn in the river's course about six miles upstream from our crossing point, the Americans emplaced cannon and stretched a 165-ton, 1,000-link chain across the river, halting the enemy vessels.

Once across the river, the trail follows for a short time the old road that led to Benedict Arnold's headquarters opposite West Point. American troops escorted Maj. John André, Arnold's British accomplice, to prison along this road.

Since 1802 the United States Military Academy has stood on the heights overlooking the Hudson at West Point. We visited the academy one scorching afternoon in August, arriving just in time for the annual

Presentation Review when upperclassmen officially welcome plebes, or first-year men, into the Corps of Cadets.

On the bright green Plain more than 3,800 young men stood at starched attention, ranks of plebes facing companies of upperclassmen. At bellowed commands the band sounded off and columns of cadets marched across the field, the plebes neatly merging for the first time with their assigned companies. Then they continued past the reviewing stand, snapping heads and eyes to the right.

A FEW DAYS LATER, in Connecticut, autumn began to catch up with us. Hot days and muggy nights had dogged us all the way from Georgia, but now we noticed a subtle change. The night air was refreshing instead of oppressive; the moon, still a month short of harvest, shone so brightly it kept us awake and turned familiar forest shapes into dreamworld phantoms. And the unseen crickets and katydids, those harbingers of fall, began their nightly concerts — steady-pitched singing that flowed back and forth across the campground.

We came upon a beaver dam, by chance the first we had seen, although beavers live as far south as Alabama. In the bog behind the dam, quacking ducks paddled through a fuzzy maze of gray cattails. The beaver lodge was so symmetrical it might have come from an upended salad mold.

Near Cornwall, the trail passes through a virgin stand of white pines a hundred feet tall, appropriately called Cathedral Pines. Even the birds and chipmunks seem subdued in the quiet majesty of the place. Soft shadows and deep pine needles carpeted the forest floor.

Just beyond Cathedral Pines we fell into conversation with a couple on the trail — Mike Jacubouis, a thoughtful, pipe-smoking director of vocational education in the state school for delinquent boys in Portland, Maine, and tall, blond Cara Perkins, an outdoors enthusiast from Cornwall. We learned they were planning to be married at Cathedral Pines, and we gladly accepted an invitation to attend the ceremony.

The Saturday of the wedding, about 60 of us assembled in Mohawk State Forest, wearing "comfortable hiking clothes" as the invitation had suggested. The bride and groom were in denim shirts and sturdy knickers with bright red suspenders, and they both wore climbing boots; Mike's stainless-steel drinking cup swung at his belt.

In a small clearing beneath a pine tree, the Reverend Bill Kittredge of Lewiston, Maine — the "hiking preacher," the invitation had called him — read from Henry David Thoreau's *Walden:*

"We need the tonic of wildness — to wade sometimes in marshes where the bittern and the meadow-hen lurk, and hear the booming of the snipe; to smell the whispering sedge where only some wilder and more solitary fowl builds her nest, and the mink crawls with its belly close to the ground. . . . We can never have enough of nature. We must be refreshed by the sight of inexhaustible vigor, vast and titanic features, the sea-coast with its wrecks, the wilderness with its living and its decaying trees, the thundercloud, and the rain which lasts three weeks and produces freshets. We need to witness our own limits transgressed, and some life pasturing freely where we never wander."

Then we set out, up the gentle incline of Mohawk Mountain. I walked awhile beside Cara, and asked why she had chosen the Appalachian Trail for her wedding place.

"Simply because wilderness is so important to Mike and me," she said. "It's a very big part of our lives. We both hike a lot with the Appalachian Mountain Club, and occasionally lead hikes; so it seemed natural to us to have our friends join us in the kind of setting we both love, and to be married here."

We reached the summit of Mohawk, and the bride and groom and their families gathered on a low stone observation tower while the rest of us sat on the grass. As soon as several romping dogs could be quieted, the ceremony continued with melodies played on recorders, the flute-like tones lingering low and clear in the still air. For several minutes no one stirred.

After the company sang two folk songs, accompanied by guitar and banjo, the hiking preacher read these words of Thoreau:

"I never asked thy leave to let me love thee—I have a right.... O how I think of you! You are purely good—you are infinitely good.... I did not think that humanity was so rich."

Again we walked. As we neared Cathedral Pines we met a troop of Boy Scouts from Pound Ridge, New York, who were thunderstruck to find themselves momentarily in the midst of a wedding party.

As we took seats on the fragrant pine needles and the guitarist strummed the chords of "God of Our Fathers," the bridegroom's 84-year-old grandmother joined us. She had made the short but steep hike from the opposite direction, and arrived scarcely out of breath, murmuring exultantly in a Polish accent, "I make it! I make it!"

Now Mike and Cara stood side by side, facing us, to exchange their vows. Above them the pines, moving gently in a slight breeze, sounded like someone's soft breathing as the service concluded:

May the silence of the hills,
The joy of the winds,
The peace of the fields,
The music of the birds,
The fire of the sun,
The strength of the trees,
And the faith of you—
In all of which is God—
Be in your hearts.

Broadly smiling friends formed an archway of ice axes for the newlyweds as they left the grove. We walked the mile or so to the bride's home, and joined in a reception on the lawn.

A few days later at the Miles Wildlife Sanctuary, about three miles off the trail near Sharon, Connecticut, we heard a sound like the honking of a circus clown's taxicab: A solitary Canada goose was circling the lake. John Anderson, the hearty national director of the Audubon Society's Research and Sanctuary Division, welcomed us into his home on the refuge.

"I can't remember a time when I wasn't interested in birds," he told us. "Born that way, I guess." The 600-acre Miles refuge is one of 45 that the Audubon Society maintains in various parts of the country. Some also serve as nature study centers. "Teachers attend workshops here," John explained, "and we help them find ways of using the out-of-doors as a classroom. Naturalists, too, receive on-the-job training.

"The Audubon Society first came into the news back in 1904 when it began trying to save the American egret. Guy Bradley, our first warden at the Lake Cuthbert rookery in Florida—now a part of Everglades National Park—was murdered by plume hunters when he tried to stop them from shooting nesting egrets."

He told us about a dilemma he was facing: an overpopulation of deer on some refuges. "For example, there are 250 on one 1,800-acre refuge—way too many. But what can we do? To let in hunters violates the concept of a sanctuary. If we feed them, we're merely making the problem worse. But to sit back and watch them starve is heartbreaking.

"We're considering the possibility of periodic, rigidly controlled harvests by hunters. We're also trying to increase the supply of deer browse, and where possible we encourage the large predators such as wolves and mountain lions."

Near Falls Village, Connecticut, the trail comes within a mile of Music Mountain, summer home of the Berkshire String Quartet. The famed chamber group's season was over, but we attended a performance by the visiting Dessoff Singers from New York.

Founder of Music Mountain in 1929 was the late Jacques Gordon, a violinist who acquired 117 acres on the mountaintop and built four cottages and a recital hall. Backpackers in shorts and jeans and well-dressed concertgoers from Hartford and New York eyed each other somewhat uncertainly as they shared pews in the hall, which seats 300. It was designed to duplicate the acoustical properties of a violin, and enfolded us in the warm sound of *a cappella* music by 17th-century composers.

The crossing of the trail from Connecticut into Massachusetts at Sages Ravine is a charming walk. Curving among jumbled rocks, a fern-bordered stream tumbled along beside us, down into the moist, cool, dark ravine—a proper place, it seemed, for a friendly troll. Mossy stones paved the stream bed, and a strange, pale fungus grew at the base of the trees. The cheerful chatter of the stream drowned out all other sounds except an occasional *chick-a-dee-dee-dee* from the lower branches of a hemlock.

The trail winds through the handsome Berkshire Hills and for a third time crosses the Housatonic River, the stream that flowed past Herman Melville's window near Pittsfield as he wrote *Moby Dick*.

We were attracted to Great Barrington by signs of preparation for the annual community fair, a week-long festival that features horse racing as well as the traditional exhibits and carnival. The fair has been an annual event since the 1840's.

The rides along the midway hadn't changed much from the kind that made me queasy as a boy. But the expected calliope music, if it was playing at all, was completely submerged by the ruthlessly amplified chords of two rock groups competing in the Battle of the Bands. My ears throbbed and my head ached, but the teen-agers around me, busy with sticky pink swirls of cotton candy, seemed completely unperturbed by the deluge of sound.

Inside the exhibit barns, rows and rows of shelves displayed prize-winning cakes and pies, pickles and preserves, fruits and vegetables, and dried flower arrangements. One shed presented—for an admission fee of 50 cents—"Black Jack, the world's largest steer," weighing 3,400 pounds and measuring 6 feet high at the shoulders and 11 feet from nose to tail. Pens of trimmed, laundered sheep, wearing canvas body stockings to keep them clean, bleated as if in amusement at the passing parade of humans.

At the grandstand and track, serious business was going on: Horses from throughout the country raced every afternoon, and a block-long line of betting windows stayed busy as farmers, townspeople, and visitors— conspicuous in pants suits and sport coats—hurried to wager between races.

T HE NOISE and activity of Great Barrington seemed far away as we climbed Mount Greylock. At 3,491 feet it is the highest peak in Massachusetts, and its "hoary aspect in winter," says the trail guidebook, accounts for its name. It has been the center of the 11,000-acre Greylock State Reservation since 1898.

At its summit stands a curious monument, a stone tower topped by an onion-shaped dome. It is dedicated to Massachusetts' war dead, but the neglected structure is crumbling and signs reading *Danger—Keep Out* have been posted.

Greylock reminded me—as it has other hikers—of the Smokies. The Appalachian Trail again becomes a tunnel, roofed with the dense branches of trees; here they are spruce, fir, and assorted hardwoods. Once this forest was chestnuts, beeches, and white pines where flocks of passenger pigeons roosted. But the chestnuts succumbed to the blight, beeches were harvested for railroad ties, and both beeches and pines were taken for mine timbers and charcoal. There were once 38 tanneries and 185 sawmills in the Berkshires, and the trees fell for them in uncounted thousands.

Ski trails slice down the sides of Greylock, but so far no ski tows have been built. An organization called the Mount Greylock Protective Association, assisted by the Appalachian Mountain Club and other conservation organizations, has successfully kept developers off the state lands.

Before leaving Massachusetts we visited Mrs. Fred W. Hutchinson, surely one of the state's most gracious citizens. Mrs. Hutchinson's home in the town of Washington is half a mile from a lean-to in the October Mountain State Forest, and she is mentioned in the trail guidebook: "Brook in rear of lean-to unsafe for drinking; obtain spring water from Mrs. Hutchinson's home 0.67 m. north."

The two-story frame house is very old, and sits beside what was once a route of the Boston-Albany Turnpike. A porch runs the length of the front of the house, which served turnpike travelers as a station for changing horses. A small plaque near the front door reads *1811*. "That's not right," said Mrs. Hutchinson. "That's just the earliest record."

With a no-nonsense cordiality she hurried us into her parlor, out of the chill autumn weather. The flames snapped and danced hospitably behind the glass front of the pot-bellied wood stove. Lace curtains bordered the windows, and family photographs and watercolors of wild flowers— painted by Mrs. Hutchinson—hung on the walls. It was a cozy, delightfully pleasant room.

When she had served us coffee and cookies, Mrs. Hutchinson showed us the scrapbook and register she has been keeping since 1938. Hikers who stop for water are asked to sign the register, and those attempting the entire trail get a red star. The scrapbook held postcards, letters, clippings, and photographs, many picturing her with pack-laden hikers. "I don't see how anybody who lives along the trail can fail to be grateful for it," she said as she recalled the friends who had first come to her door as strangers. "It is a privilege to meet people with eyes to see beauty."

We had arrived at Mrs. Hutchinson's home because of a misunderstanding; we had incorrectly interpreted an entry in the guidebook to mean that hikers could find accommodations at Washington's town hall, and that Mrs. Hutchinson was the person to see about such arrangements.

"Oh, no," she said, "my, no. That's wrong." Not only was the old town hall not a hostel, but the Sons and Daughters of Washington had only recently succeeded in saving it from destruction and were beginning to restore it. Already they had given it a new coat of paint. She was pleased that they had been able in this case to foil "the modern mania" for tearing down old buildings. "If the wind takes it down, so be it," she said, "but let us not be the wind."

After some hesitation, Mrs. Hutchinson agreed to read to us from a memoir she had written called "Home on the Trail."

"It's not for publication," she explained, "not even for quotation. It's for my family, so they'll know what it has meant to me to live here on the trail." In a low, steady voice, she read to us of the joys and trials of rearing a large and active family; of her husband, who had been dean of engineering at a branch of Northeastern University; of sons who had gone off to war; of hikers who had stopped for water and had become lifelong friends.

Hearing her account was a lovely and moving experience. It provided one of our fondest memories of the entire journey.

Had Mrs. Hutchinson ever hiked any of the trail?

"Just once," she smiled. "And then I wasn't really hiking. Just picking wild flowers on Bald Mountain."

As we took our leave, Mrs. Hutchinson followed us out onto the lawn, and gazed affectionately and thoughtfully at her home.

"It will not last forever," she said. "Any more than I will. Or you. Or anyone else."

From her journal "Home on the Trail," Mrs. Fred W. Hutchinson reads to a visitor.

"*It is a privilege to meet people with eyes to see beauty.*"

"The music of the birds, the strength of the trees... be in your hearts."

After their wedding on the trail, Mike and Cara Jacubouis leave Cathedral Pines through an archway of ice axes. The couple first met on an Appalachian Mountain Club canoe trip; they and most of their guests belong to the club. As part of the ceremony near Cornwall Village, Connecticut, the party hiked over Mohawk Mountain to this virgin stand of white pines, pausing occasionally to sing and to listen to guitar and recorder music and readings from Henry David Thoreau. At upper left, members of a young people's church fellowship splash in Lake Marcia in New Jersey's High Point State Park; beyond them, a monument marks the state's top elevation: 1,803 feet. On the wide, level trail to Sunfish Pond, New Jersey, two girls move in for the weekend.

From the Delaware Water Gap to the Vermont line, the trail passes through several state forests, parks, and wildlife preserves, as well as private land. One of the most popular sections crosses Harriman and Bear Mountain State Parks, part of the Palisades Interstate Park system. Hikers can visit Bear Mountain's Trailside Museum and explore many nature paths. Deer and beavers inhabit the Audubon Wildlife Center and Miles Wildlife Sanctuary near Sharon, Connecticut. Music Mountain presents concerts by the Berkshire String Quartet; Tanglewood provides a summer home for the Boston Symphony Orchestra; and Jacob's Pillow offers ballet performances. A day's hike leads to the highest point in the rolling Berkshire Hills, the 3,491-foot summit of Mount Greylock. This 300-mile stretch ends near Williamstown, Massachusetts, where Williams College opened in 1793.

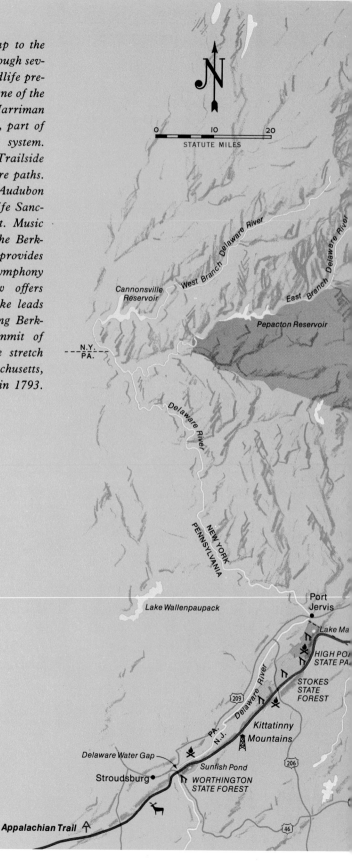

□   Point of interest

Campground

Trail shelter

Wildlife refuge

Fire tower

Deer in vicinity

Foxes in vicinity

Beavers in vicinity

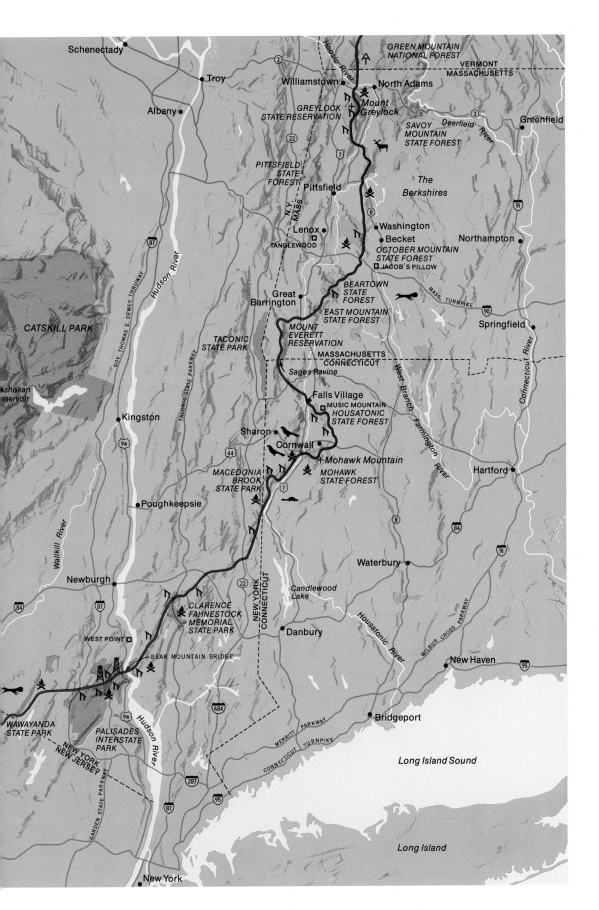

Red-spotted newt, a common New England salamander, crawls on a moist rock. The autumn frost has shattered an aster's symmetry (right). Water striders search for smaller insect prey. Below, a beaver lodge dominates its pond near Manchester, Vermont.

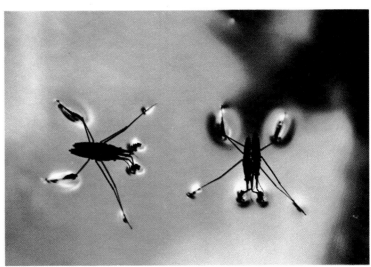

Enduring and durable summer favorite, Arthur Fiedler conducts the Boston Pops Orchestra at Tanglewood, a former estate near Lenox, Massachusetts. At another concert, thousands of rock music fans listen to a Contemporary Trends program. For eight weeks in July and August, Tanglewood presents the Berkshire Festival, with performances by the Boston Symphony, members of the Berkshire Music Center, and other musicians. Attendance for all events in 1972 exceeded 225,000.

Morning sun burns mist off the Hudson; the United States Military Academy, established at West Point, New York, in 1802, lies at lower right along the river. During the Presentation Review (below) on an August afternoon, four regiments of upperclassmen on the far side of the parade ground welcome 1,360 plebes into the Corps of Cadets. Families and friends watch from the bleachers.

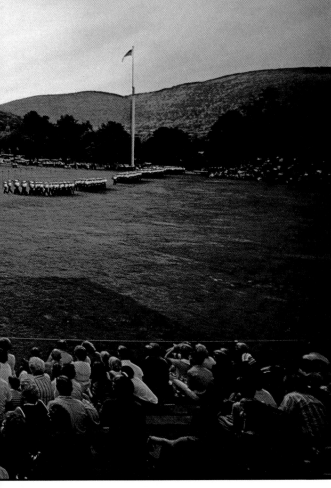

7.

New England's pathway through the clouds

A T LITTLE ROCK POND in Vermont, the annual pageant of the leaves was just beginning; here and there among the trees a splotch of bright color offered a hint of the coming extravaganza. The setting of the pond seemed to me one of the loveliest on the trail. An air of serenity surrounded it like the circle of warmth around a campfire. Near one end a short wooden bridge led to an island just big enough for a few trees, some boulders and shrubs, and a shelter.

Three hairy young hippies had been living in the shelter for several days, and I—an old-timer on the wrong side of 30—hesitated to intrude on their idyll. But they immediately made me welcome. They were soft-spoken dropouts who spent their days feeding peanut butter to the chipmunks, swimming in the pond, and paddling around on a small rubber raft. One had just acquired his first fishing license but had no gear to his name, so he asked to borrow my tackle. He quickly caught a couple of trout, whose glossy, speckled skins flashed in the sun as they flopped on the rocks. But it disturbed the novice angler and his friends to see the fish suffer, so he put the tackle away. Thoreau asked, "Who hears the fishes when they cry?" These young men heard.

In the evening we played cards in the flickering light of an old lantern. During the night an owl on the opposite shore hooted softly, and the reassuring call floated across the water like a watchman's "all's well."

Next morning the hippies moved on, and I spent most of the day alone on the rocks at the water's edge, cloud-gazing, pond-watching, listening to insects buzzing nearby, feeling the sun's warmth on my face and back. The Green Mountains, verdant as their name suggests, rose all around me.

Rigid with rime ice, sedge gleams near the summit of Mount Washington, New Hampshire. Here, 20-degree cold and 70-mile-an-hour wind chilled the hikers as much as would a calm day at 23 below zero.

Green Mountain National Forest encloses 242,000 acres of the range, stretching northward 110 miles—with a break in the middle—from the Massachusetts border to 4,135-foot Mount Ellen. The trail runs through the national forest as far as Sherburne Pass, where it turns northeast toward New Hampshire.

The wooded slopes are almost entirely second-growth forest again covering much-abused land. Early settlers cut and burned thousands of trees to obtain potash, used in the manufacture of soap and glass; at one time a bushel of ashes was more valuable than a bushel of wheat. That demand ended when sodium, more easily obtained, replaced potash. Then white pine, spruce, oak, and hemlock fell to the lumbering industry; hemlock was also sought for its tannin. And blight took the chestnut trees.

Sheep, too, posed a serious threat here once. At the height of the sheep boom, around 1840, the animals outnumbered people in Vermont six to one. Where sheep graze intensively, erosion soon follows, for their hoofs are sharp and they eat grass down close to the soil; these hills might have turned into a wasteland. But after 1865, Vermont sheep were raised primarily for breeding stock to build herds in the West, Australia, and South America, and the large flocks dwindled.

Today old sheep pastures and former potash and charcoal acreage are again producing mixed stands of brush, conifers, and hardwoods, and in time the forests of Vermont should resemble their original condition.

In the 18th century this region was made famous by Ethan Allen and his Green Mountain Boys, who served colorfully in the Revolutionary War. A braggart and a bully, Allen wore gaudy uniforms of his own design and affected grand titles. His army consisted of about 200 straight-shooting fighters from the hills and hollows.

Their most heralded exploit took them to British-held Fort Ticonderoga on the shores of Lake Champlain, which they stormed on May 10, 1775. Allen demanded "in the name of the great Jehovah and the Continental Congress" that the commander surrender. He complied.

When the Appalachian Trail enters Vermont it merges for 94 miles with the Long Trail, a 262-mile path that runs the length of the state from Massachusetts to Canada. It was the idea and the achievement of James P. Taylor, associate principal of the Vermont Academy.

In 1909 Taylor tried to lead a group of students to the top of Pico Peak, but the thick brush cover defeated them. Determined to make the highlands more accessible, Taylor began agitating for a trail through the Green Mountains. He spoke before every group that would give him a few minutes at the podium, from Bible classes to businessmen's conventions. Of the thousands in his audience, a few listened, and in 1910 about two dozen gathered to form the Green Mountain Club and start planning the trail.

The founders went to work organizing regional clubs that would work on sections of the trail. The first portion was the 29 miles between Camels Hump and Smugglers Notch, just north of Mount Mansfield. In 1931 the Long Trail was completed.

Green Mountain Club members have been prolific shelter builders: Between the Massachusetts line and Sherburne Pass, the structures average one every three and a half miles.

When winter turns these mountains from green to white, skiers arrive by the thousand. At Bromley Mountain the trail ascends side by side with a novice ski trail, crossing the summit near the upper station of the chair lift. Imagine our surprise to find there—in September, with the grass still green—a hillside swarming with skiers! Mounted on grass skis, which move over the turf on small rollers, they were warming up for the Grass Ski Championships.

An accomplished skier on snow, Dick tried the new gear, developed in the mid-1960's. Somewhat battered, he rendered this summary report: "I thought it would be a snap. But it isn't as easy as it looks!"

FROM THE TOP of one mountain we descended deep into another, to see what underlies the trail at this point. The Vermont Marble Company has been extracting stone from Danby Mountain since 1905, superintendent Bill Smith told us as he handed out bright yellow hard hats. Through a hole about 20 feet wide we entered the mountain to find ourselves in an L-shaped cavern the size of a stadium.

It was early morning and the workmen were just arriving. Bill led us down a long flight of wooden steps to the sloping floor of the cavern. Passageways opened into galleries as large as gymnasiums. Light bulbs strung along the ceiling lit the way as we continued our descent, past marble pillars left to support the 300 feet of mountain above us. A small gray shadow darted behind one of these. "A cat," said Bill. "Several live down here and never go out. The men feed them from their lunches."

Two shifts totaling 60 men work comfortably in the cool 47-degree temperature, which remains constant year around. At a sharp blast of a whistle, the workday began—and so did the noise. Compressors to power air drills started up, and a bulldozer began to move rubble. Conversation was impossible between people more than a couple of feet apart, and the men used hand signals to communicate.

A muffled explosion made the floor tremble, and I glanced toward the ceiling. "Don't worry," Bill shouted. "Marble excavations are the soundest in the world. They may fill up with water, but they'll never cave in."

The quarrymen loosened each block of marble by outlining a square section with drill holes. There was a moment of uneasiness when a 16-ton block was ready to move; an inch-and-a-half cable from a derrick was snaked around it, then everyone stood back as the cable stretched taut until it hummed like a bowstring. Finally, with a groan, the block broke free, and a huge forklift loaded it onto a flatbed truck.

"Marble weighs 180 pounds a cubic foot," said Bill, "and we've taken out blocks as big as 83 tons. This is the largest underground white-marble quarry in the world."

On the porch of the Happy Hill Cabin near West Hartford, I realized winter was coming. As I sat with a cup of coffee late in the chill afternoon, a small blue butterfly landed on the sleeve of my jacket with the lightness of a snowflake. I watched it for a moment, then gently exhaled my warm breath in its direction. The butterfly wriggled its long antennae, danced in a little circle—and edged closer. I blew another breath, and it tiptoed farther up my arm. The black eyes seemed to regard me with pleasure and gratitude, and the butterfly moved back and forth, circling and returning, as long as I would cooperate. We played our strange little game for more than ten minutes, until I reluctantly sent my visitor off to an uncertain destiny. A couple of nights later the temperature dipped below freezing, and I saw no more butterflies.

Happy Hill Cabin sits on a hundred-acre parcel of land owned by Dartmouth College, and before we left, Earl Jette, lecturer in environmental studies, arrived to inspect the place. "I'm planning to bring my students up here for some field classes," he explained.

Earl is also assistant director of the Dartmouth Outing Club. "A Dartmouth undergraduate named Fred H. Harris formed the club in 1910," he recounted. "He saw a need for the students to get outdoors, to explore some of the natural wonders of the area.

"The members went skiing in winter, and hiking and camping in spring and fall. They began building cabins—there are now 11 that Dartmouth owns and maintains.

"Today the club has about 1,100 members—not all of them active—in several divisions. The division concerned with cabins and trails maintains about 75 miles of the Appalachian Trail—from Vermont Highway 12 to Kinsman Notch—and also a network of loop trails."

Four miles from Happy Hill we crossed the Connecticut River—along with the traffic on Vermont Highway 10A—and entered Hanover, New Hampshire. The trail follows West Wheelock Street up a hill to the Dartmouth College green. Students, long accustomed to seeing heavily laden backpackers pass through the center of their campus, ignored us. Three touch-football games were in progress, students were sprawled on the grass studying, and a black German shepherd was showing off his skill at leaping into the air and catching a Frisbee.

Handsome old buildings surrounded the green, and the three comprising Dartmouth Row especially interested me. Hugh Morrison, a former professor of art at the college, had written: "With perfect repose and integrity, Dartmouth Hall achieved an architectural distinction.... It is particularly fortunate in its setting and in the harmonious grouping of its near neighbors, Wentworth and Thornton Halls...."

Professor Morrison, now retired, agreed to escort me on a tour around the green. We paused before the three-storied Dartmouth Hall, from the roof of which rises an ornate cupola housing the college bell. "This was for a number of years the sole edifice of Dartmouth College," my distinguished guide said. "It was erected just after the Revolution, between 1784 and 1791. It has burned and been rebuilt twice.

"Dartmouth was the ninth college established in the Colonies," he continued. "It received its royal charter from George III in 1769 as a school for Indians, but the charter allowed also for the education 'of English Youth and any others.' Dr. Eleazar Wheelock chose the site here in 1770. He started with six Indians.

"One ex-student who would interest you is John Ledyard, who entered Dartmouth in 1772 but was bored, so dropped out and signed on with Captain Cook for one voyage. Off the Pacific Northwest coast he conceived the idea of hiking across northern Europe and Asia toward Alaska. He made it from Hamburg, Germany, to Irkutsk in Siberia before Catherine the Great had him deported as a spy.

"While at Dartmouth he canoed down the Connecticut River to Long Island Sound; now every year, members of the Ledyard Canoe Club make the same trip."

We got our first look at New Hampshire's White Mountains from the summit of Mount Moosilauke, as the sun set behind us over Vermont. We arrived just at dusk, after a steep two-hour climb, and gazed out at the range before us. Here were neither the rounded humps of the southern Appalachians nor the rolling hills of the middle Atlantic states, but rugged, belligerent peaks encircled by squadrons of threatening clouds.

Woolen stocking-caps pulled down over our ears, we leaned into the howling wind and tried to keep our balance. The naked boulders seemed an unlikely site for a building, but in fact several lodges were constructed here by 1860 and a carriage road led all the way up to them.

Four hundred feet down the slope we shared a cabin with three other hikers, two young men coming south from Mount Katahdin and a young silversmith from Dover, New Hampshire. His trail companion was a puppy, Maria, who scrambled happily over the rocks to bark at the big gray rabbits that loped through the scrawny brush.

The night passed without a recurrence of Jill's experience of a week before. In the middle of a foggy night alone here, she had heard the wind blow open the door to admit a lumbering creature — probably a porcupine — that shuffled through the cabin exploring every corner and cranny. "I was too scared even to reach for my flashlight," she said.

New England's mountain ranges are primarily composed of greatly altered rocks that originated on the sea bottom 500 million to 200 million years ago. A series of geologic upheavals folded and fractured them, finally transforming them into slate, marble, and schist. Along with the geologic spasms, plutonic activity injected masses of molten rock, none more prominent than the huge granitic concentrations making up the Presidential Range of the White Mountains.

For the last 200 million years, the New England ranges have been undergoing attacks by erosional processes, including glaciation. It was only some 15,000 years ago that the last glacial stage ended, leaving deposits of sand, gravel, and erratic boulders.

The last glacier sculptured the profile of an old man by gouging several different ledges of granite. Not far from the trail the Old Man of the Mountain broods over Franconia Notch.

One of the Old Man's shoulders is Cannon Mountain, whose sheer cliff at the highway through the notch attracts nimble rock climbers. We joined three members of the Dartmouth Mountaineering Club, a division of the Outing Club, one Saturday early in October. Budge Gierke, Chris Walker, and John Cleary, laden with ropes and clattering with pitons and karabiners, led us up a talus slope to the base of the cliff. Other climbers already dotted the rock face like bugs pinned to a board.

Jill had done some climbing in the West and elected to go with the three men. In pairs they started up the Whitney-Gilman route, named for the first climbers to negotiate it. John, first up, moved slowly, driving a

piton about every 20 feet or wedging a nut into a crevice, clipping his rope to these anchors while Budge kept it tight from the ground. After climbing about 40 feet he found a ledge, secured the rope, and called for Budge to come up. As the second man climbed he removed the pitons and nuts while John kept the rope tight. Then the second couple started.

It was a tedious process. They inched their way upward, reaching for handholds, looking for footholds. A quarter of a mile away, another climber had a harmonica secured by a wire harness around his neck, and as he waited on a ledge for his partner he improvised a melancholy tune.

Dick and I watched through binoculars until Jill and her companions had moved out of sight beyond a hump in the cliff. Then we drove to the other side of the mountain and took an aerial tramway to the top.

While we waited there, I talked to a couple of climbers who arrived ahead of Jill's group: Brad Schramm and Bill Galvin, the harmonica player. "It's kind of boring sometimes, waiting for your partner," Bill said, "so I like to have the harmonica to pass the time."

When I asked about the fascination of rock climbing, Bill answered: "It's not just a matter of getting to the top; it's *how* you get there. In some spots there's only one way to do it. When you've made it, you know you've done something perfect. It's you against the rocks."

Were they ever scared? "Sure," said Brad, "but if you're shaky scared, you don't have any energy and you can't do anything. You're with your fear all the time at first. Then you forget about being scared and just think about the rocks."

Early in North American history sailors tacking along the coast of New England reported a massive mountain range well inland. Capt. John Smith spotted one glittering peak he called "the twinkling mountaine." It was probably Mount Washington, highest peak of the Presidential Range. Seven Presidential summits rise above 5,000 feet; Washington reaches 6,288. Here the Appalachian Trail becomes a pathway through the clouds, crossing all the major peaks.

The first white man to climb Mount Washington was an immigrant

"Before dark, we sometimes found time for a few hands of canasta."

from Boston, England, named Darby Field, who made two ascents in 1642. He hired several Indians to accompany him, but as they neared the summit the Indians grew fearful, believing it to be the home of the Great Spirit; only two agreed to make the final push to the top. From there Field saw what he thought was a large body of water—it turned out to be cloudbanks—and sheets of mica he reported to be 40 feet long and 8 feet wide, a considerable exaggeration. There is abundant mica, however, that may account for the twinkling that John Smith saw. About a month later, Darby climbed Washington again, descending jubilantly with large stones imbedded with "diamonds" that turned out to be quartz.

There was no route through the White Mountains until 1771, when a moose hunter named Timothy Nash climbed a tree to get his bearings and saw an opening in the wall of rock. He hurried with his news to the royal governor at Portsmouth. "Bring a horse down the pass," the governor instructed, "and show me that it will be a practicable route for the settlers, and you shall have a grant of land." Nash needed rope and tackle—and a partner named Sawyer—to get his horse down one ledge, but met the challenge and won his reward: 2,184 acres.

In 1792 the Crawford family—Abel, Hannah, and their two sons, Ethan Allen and Erastus—settled near the Nash-Sawyer property. There was room for farming, and the Saco River provided water power; but the homestead was on what turned out to be the principal route through the White Mountains, so Abel turned innkeeper. For the next 30 years he and his family built inns and blazed trails; atop Mount Washington they erected three stone shelters.

We began our climb toward Washington on a trail that touches U. S. Highway 302 in Crawford Notch, near the site of one of the Crawford family's inns. Just inside the cover of trees we found a sign: "Crawford Path—the Oldest Continuously Used Mountain Trail in America. In 1819 Abel Crawford and his son Ethan Allen cleared this path to treeline near the top of Mt. Clinton. . . . Countless thousands have traveled this path to the Presidential Range and Mt. Washington."

Two privately funded organizations—the Society for the Protection of New Hampshire Forests and the Appalachian Mountain Club—have worked with energy and dedication for many years to protect the White Mountains and help make them accessible. Along with its trail work the AMC has built a string of nine "huts"—a misleading name, for they are really hostels that accommodate from 36 to 100 in dormitory-style rooms and have a staff of young people on hand to prepare meals.

We tramped into the Mizpah Spring Hut, 3,800 feet high on Mount Clinton, late in the afternoon. Built in 1964, it is solid and spacious and can sleep 60 hikers. All its food supplies are backpacked in from the highway, two and a half miles down the mountain, by the staff.

We found the hut overflowing with seventh-graders from the Frank A. Day Junior High School in Newton, Massachusetts.

"Few of these kids have ever been backpacking before," said Michael Cohen, the enthusiastic young consultant with the Newton school system who was helping to coordinate this experiment in outdoor education. "They're surprised that we make them carry their litter with them. They cleaned up the top of Mount Jackson this morning."

I learned this was not a new program. "In two years we've brought 300 kids up here for three-day hikes," Mike said. "We try to teach them an integrated program—including science, ecology, map reading. We help them learn how plants adapt, where the different birds and animals live, where various types of rocks protrude. We encourage them to help the teachers find these things. They learn more in three days in the woods than in three weeks in a classroom."

They were a well-behaved group of youngsters as they seated themselves at rows of tables in the dining room. Propane lanterns hanging from the ceiling lighted the long room.

I sat down beside John Nutter, the rugged, bearded Appalachian Mountain Club officer in charge of educational programs. John conducts the workshops that prepare science teachers for the rigors of leading groups of children through the White Mountains. He told me about his organization, the oldest hiking association in America.

"We have a membership of about 16,000 now," he said. "The club was organized in 1876 to explore the mountains of New England and to generate interest in the geography and preservation of the region. Today we have the same problem in this area that they're having in some of the national parks: abuses by too many insensitive people. We're trying several new ideas. We don't plan to build any more huts or shelters, but rather to establish camping areas with tent platforms, and hire resident managers to keep an eye on things. The Forest Service may have to limit the number of hikers by issuing permits.

"The AMC maintains about 350 miles of trails in the White Mountains, including a hundred miles or so of the Appalachian Trail. We have a summer trail crew of 24 high school and college kids. They start out at $38 a week plus room and board, and work from June into September.

"Then we have these nine huts to manage. Each has a hut master and a crew of hut boys who work with him. Mizpah is kind of an exception: Have you met our first hut girl?"

Twice a week Cathy Ferree would hike down to the highway, she informed me, to meet a truck, load her pack board with 60 or 70 pounds of groceries and other supplies, and make the grueling climb back to Mizpah. "I packed 80 pounds once and about died," she said.

Dana Whiting, the hut master, is a physical education graduate of the University of Bridgeport. He became interested in the hut system through a brother, and worked his way up from hut boy.

A hut crew has a busy schedule. "We take turns doing the cooking," Cathy explained after the supper dishes had been washed and put away with the help of a brigade of seventh-grade driers. "The cook plans the menu. We're usually up by six to start breakfast. The guests get up at six-thirty.

"After people have checked out we have our breakfast, clean the place up, make the trip for supplies — if necessary — and haul out the garbage. We set ourselves some general maintenance job every day. By four it's time to start the evening meal. After supper we pack trail lunches for anyone who wants them the next day, and at eight there's tea. Lights go out at ten. It keeps us jumping, but we love it."

Dana added a comment. "Some people get on our nerves a little bit. They show up here in pants suits and sneakers on their way up Mount Washington, without any idea of what they're getting into. We have to persuade them to go back. We also have to try to get people to pick up their litter. And when people get lost or break a leg, it's the hut boys who go after them and carry them down off the mountain. It happens several times a season. I don't think people realize that when they come to the Presidentials unprepared — when they start out in bad weather, or without knowing what they're doing — and get themselves in trouble, other people are going to have to risk their lives rescuing them."

AFTER BREAKFAST next morning one group of the seventh-graders seated themselves at the tables for a lesson in map reading. "All right," said Mike, "how do we know if there's water on the trail?" Thirty heads bowed over crinkled AMC maps. "The blue lines are rivers," offered one boy. "Right," said Mike. "Now how many rivers will we cross on our way to Zealand Falls Hut?" Thirty fingers inched along the route. "Three," somebody said.

Outside, another group led by Judy Andrucki was ready to set out, and we followed along in the clean, fresh morning air. Soon Judy, a biology teacher, called out, "Look what's happening to the trees." Indeed, the tree pattern was changing, for an ascent of the higher Presidentials is roughly the same in terms of climate variation as a trip 1,550 miles northward to the Arctic Circle. At the base of the mountain we had hiked through a hardwood forest of maples, beeches, and birches, sprinkled with a few conifers. Now we began to see red spruces and balsam firs as the deciduous species thinned out.

Spongy clumps of peat moss caught Judy's eye. "When peat moss is dry it can absorb more than its own weight in water," she said. "The Indians used to dry it and put it in their babies' diapers." The class giggled.

Soon she stooped and plucked a few leaves from a low-growing plant. "These are Labrador tea leaves," she said. "We could make tea out of them just as they are, or dry them. Notice how fuzzy the bottoms are? Why do you suppose that is?" No one hazarded a guess. "To hold water," she said. "It collects in the fuzz and clings there when the wind blows."

When we reached timberline, Judy called attention to patches of black spruce, gnarled and stunted from a constant contest with the wind. We saw some that were more than a hundred years old, with trunks 15 to 20 feet long growing laterally among the rocks but never rising more than a few inches off the ground; for when growing shoots reach above the protective blanket of snow, the desiccating wind kills them. "You can see how things adapt even to the harshest environment," said Judy.

When we arrived at the bare summit of Mount Eisenhower, one girl looked behind her and sighed. "Every time I look back to where I've been, my feet hurt."

WE LEFT THE STUDENTS there, and from the top of Mount Franklin —well above timberline—we finally got a clear look at Mount Washington, only a couple of air miles away. As we watched, a gust of wind pushed aside the gray cloud hiding its uppermost peak and we glimpsed the spires of the weather observatory and television relay station. Then the cloud lowered again.

That was as much as we saw of the summit that day. Half a mile from the top, we reached a side trail leading down to Pinkham Notch, and we stopped for consultation. It was getting late; the cloud on Washington was settling lower. We recalled a sign posted near Mizpah: "The area ahead has the worst weather in America. Many have died there from exposure, even in the summer. Turn back *now* if the weather is bad."

We didn't turn back but we did turn aside, skirting the summit and starting down. Even so we misjudged the mountain, for darkness caught us barely halfway to the bottom. Out came our flashlights and we stumbled on. A slippery log sent me sprawling. At intervals a full moon appeared, but a procession of clouds brought recurring blackouts.

Somehow Dick, in the lead, kept us on the path until the flashlights gave out, and then we found ourselves wandering—how far from our route, we had no idea.

Remembering that we had crossed a ski trail, we backtracked until we reached it. Suddenly there was a wide, clear swath that headed straight down the mountain, illuminated by a moon that broke free of the clouds at that same instant. Side by side, exhausted but triumphant, we marched downhill to the hut at Pinkham Notch.

The next day I made another assault on Mount Washington, but this time I did it the easy way. In 1869 the world's first cog railroad was built to the summit. It was—and still is—something of an engineering miracle. Almost all its three-and-a-half-mile length is on trestle, and its average grade is 25 percent: For every four feet it goes forward, it climbs one foot. At one stage the grade exceeds 37 percent. Boilers on the engines are tilted so they will be approximately level when the trains are climbing.

I rode in the cabin with the engineer, and was alternately blasted with waves of heat—as the fireman shoveled coal into the firebox—and with icy winds that swirled through the open cabin. Soot blew in from the belching smokestack. Once we pulled onto a siding to let a downward-bound train pass, and twice we stopped at wooden water tanks. Finally, puffing and clattering, we came to a stop at the platform alongside Summit House. At Base Station the weather had been that of a typical fall day. Here it was winter; the peak was blanketed by snow and ice, the temperature was 20°, and the wind was gusting to 70 miles an hour. Every banister carried horizontal icicles, or "frost feathers."

Snow has fallen here in every month of the year, and averages 178 inches annually. The recorded temperature has never risen above 71°, and has plunged to 46° below zero. But it is the ferocity of the wind that leaves one gasping. The strongest wind ever measured on this planet gusted across Mount Washington in 1934 at 231 miles per hour.

Moreover, the weather can change drastically without warning. A hiker may walk in sunshine one minute and think he has been transported to Antarctica moments later.

An unimpeded view from here is rare, but when it comes it is, said P. T. Barnum himself, the "second greatest show on earth." On clear nights the glow of Montreal, 140 miles away, lights the horizon.

Head down against the wind, I hurried to the weather observatory where I found Norman Michaels and John Howe on duty. Norm was starting supper, with frequent reference to a Fannie Farmer Cookbook. He was planning a cake in honor of the last day of tourist season.

John showed me around. "The observatory was built in 1937," he told me, "and it's literally bolted to the rocks. We're not a part of the U. S. National Weather Service, though our reports go to them, but a nonprofit organization started in 1932 by men who were simply interested in learning about the weather on Mount Washington. Under contract to the Weather Service we transmit data every three hours, around the clock, on temperature, wind velocity, barometric pressure, and other conditions." Among many research and testing projects, the observatory operates a cosmic ray neutron monitor for the University of New Hampshire, and records permafrost temperature profiles extending 30 feet into the mountain.

The crew's snug quarters included a room given over to radios and meteorological equipment, a living room-library, a kitchen, and a bunk room. The men shared the building with a dog and a cat—recently and mysteriously a mother.

John and Norm were content with their isolated situation and the week-on-week-off rotation of crews. "By the time you're ready to go down to the valley, you can go," said Norm. "And by the time you've spent a week in town, you're ready to come back."

We went down to the basement, where the cosmic ray neutron monitor clicked away like an electric typewriter near long shelves loaded with stocks of food. Then we donned warm clothes and climbed a slippery-runged ladder through a trapdoor into the roof tower, where John de-iced the wind gauge. "Sometimes this has to be done every hour," he said. I surveyed the harsh white world around us. At least 22 people have died in the Presidentials from exposure.

The train whistle summoned me. From the railway as we descended I could see the road, opened in 1861, that climbs Mount Washington from the other side. It crosses a bridge named for Jenny Lind; the Swedish Nightingale once ordered her carriage stopped there so she could admire the view, and was so enthralled that she burst into song.

From Mount Washington the trail crosses the peaks named Clay, Jefferson, Adams, and Madison, eventually stairsteps downward, crosses the Androscoggin River, and reaches the Maine border.

The Androscoggin was once an important waterway for the logging industry. For years masts for British ships came from the pines of New England, some so enormous that a single tree would require 20 teams of oxen to haul it out of the woods.

Today the Brown Company of Berlin, New Hampshire, owns and manages several hundred thousand acres of New Hampshire and Maine. Ken Norcott, chief forester, escorted us along the part of the trail that crosses Brown land.

We saw skidders—tough, double-jointed little tractors—roaring out of the woods, dragging cut logs to the trucking area. We watched in amazement—and sadness—as a young man with a chain saw approached an 80-year-old white birch and in 58 seconds sent it crashing to the ground—perhaps for some furniture we would buy?

We ate at the company's Clear Stream Camp with about two dozen French-Canadian loggers, most of whom spoke no English, but who made room for us with smiles and courteous gestures. Most stay here only through the week, driving to their homes across the border on Friday.

On succeeding days we climbed the trail out of New Hampshire into Maine and on toward Mahoosuc Notch. The sheer granite walls of the notch were dotted with stubborn little spruces the size of small Christmas trees, whose roots had burrowed deep into cracks in the rock. The walls here are so steep that the sun shines into the notch only a few hours a day. The canyon floor is a jumble of great gray boulders spotted with green, slippery moss. We labored up the trail, ducking under projecting rocks as large as automobiles, squeezing through narrow passageways, scrambling over barriers.

Finally we stopped to rest, and I looked into a wide crack that descended far down into cool, moist twilight. At the very bottom, longer lasting than the summer now ended, was a patch of snow.

Racing against time on roller-equipped grass skis, Holly Clarke scoots through a slalom gate at Big Bromley Ski Area in Vermont. Introduced in the mid-1960's, the sport is rapidly gaining popularity.

"You're with your fear all the time at first. Then you forget about being scared and just think about the rocks."

Rock climbers tackle Cannon Cliff near Franconia, New Hampshire: from left, Budge Gierke, John Cleary, and Chris Walker. Opposite, Walker reaches for a handhold. Above, Cleary recovers a "nut" (a rope anchor) while rappelling down after the climb.

September dawn breaks over the horizon in Vermont's Green Mountain National Forest.

The trail crosses Bromley Mountain (obscured by the sun) at its 3,260-foot summit.

Standing across the Ottauquechee River from a former woolen mill, construction manager George DeVries explains Quechee Lakes Corporation's plan for Quechee, Vermont. After the last of Quechee's mills closed down in 1962, the population dwindled to 75. Now the old brick mill at upper left, partly shaded by trees, is being remodeled to house a restaurant, summer theater, and shops; the company is restoring the rest of the village, and developing some 6,000 acres as a retirement and recreation community. About half that land will remain open space. The trail borders the property for several miles. Not all Vermont mills have closed: Upstream at the Bridgewater Woolen Company, Mrs. Alna Swanson threads the harness of an automated loom that weaves complex plaids.

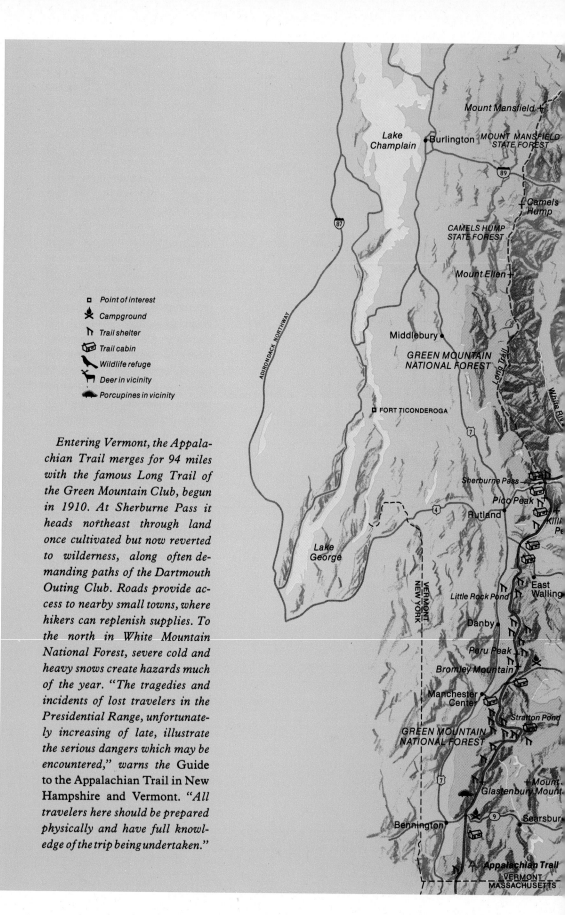

Entering Vermont, the Appalachian Trail merges for 94 miles with the famous Long Trail of the Green Mountain Club, begun in 1910. At Sherburne Pass it heads northeast through land once cultivated but now reverted to wilderness, along often demanding paths of the Dartmouth Outing Club. Roads provide access to nearby small towns, where hikers can replenish supplies. To the north in White Mountain National Forest, severe cold and heavy snows create hazards much of the year. "The tragedies and incidents of lost travelers in the Presidential Range, unfortunately increasing of late, illustrate the serious dangers which may be encountered," warns the Guide to the Appalachian Trail in New Hampshire and Vermont. "All travelers here should be prepared physically and have full knowledge of the trip being undertaken."

□ Point of interest
☆ Campground
🛖 Trail shelter
🏚 Trail cabin
🦫 Wildlife refuge
🦌 Deer in vicinity
🦔 Porcupines in vicinity

Mount Mansfield
Lake Champlain
Burlington
MOUNT MANSFIELD STATE FOREST
89
Camels Hump
CAMELS HUMP STATE FOREST
Mount Ellen
87
ADIRONDACK NORTHWAY
Middlebury
GREEN MOUNTAIN NATIONAL FOREST
Long Trail
White River
□ FORT TICONDEROGA
7
Sherburne Pass
Pico Peak
4
Rutland
Killington Peak
Lake George
East Wallingford
Little Rock Pond
VERMONT NEW YORK
Danby
Peru Peak
Bromley Mountain
Manchester Center
Stratton Pond
GREEN MOUNTAIN NATIONAL FOREST
7
Mount Glastenbury Mount
9
Searsburg
Bennington
Appalachian Trail
VERMONT
MASSACHUSETTS

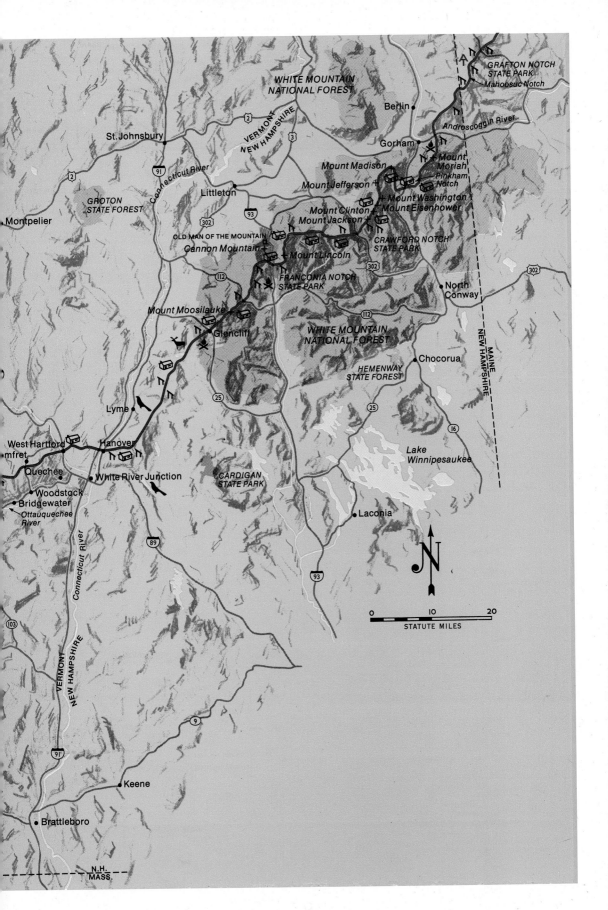

Most severe combination of wind, cold, icing, and storms recorded outside the polar regions blankets Mount Washington in white. Snow has fallen here in every month of the year, at one time or another, and wind speeds often exceed 100 mph. In its weather observatory meteorologists study extreme atmospheric conditions, as well as the clouds that mantle the peak more than half the time. Fifteen trails lead to the summit, among them the Appalachian; visitors can also reach the top by road (foreground) or by cog railway (center right, and opposite)—the world's first, completed in 1869.

"They learn more in three days
in the woods than in
three weeks in a classroom."

THE AREA AHEAD HAS THE WORST WEATHER IN AMERICA. MANY HAVE DIED THERE FROM EXPOSURE EVEN IN THE SUMMER. TURN BACK **NOW** IF THE WEATHER IS BAD.

WHITE MOUNTAIN NATIONAL FOREST

Seventh-grader Steve Rowland huddles over a map of the day's hike with Michael Cohen, environmental education consultant for the Newton, Massachusetts, school system. During three days in the White Mountains, Steve's class will learn about ecology, botany, and geology. Atop Mount Clinton, another class stops for lunch. New England teachers prepare for such outdoor programs in workshops sponsored by the Appalachian Mountain Club. The seminars stress safety, for even easy trails can quickly become hazardous. A U. S. Forest Service sign (above) warns of treacherous weather.

Skiers pack snow on a slalom course at Mount Washington's Tuckerman Ravine—in places, a 55-degree slope. At right, a youngster gets a tow during the 2½-mile hike from Pinkham Notch Camp, where the view (reflected in lodge windows) takes in the forested skyline of the White Mountains.

8.

Beyond the Kennebec to Katahdin's peak

W E TURNED OUR BACKS on a swirling blast of sand blown by the departing floatplane as it taxied away from the shore; then we faced around to watch it skim the length of Lower Jo-Mary Lake. With a dip of its tail the plane freed itself from the water, soaring up and out of our view beyond a ridge. Its roar faded to a hum, then died away, leaving us alone with the silence of the deep woods of Maine, the only sound the pontoons' wake splashing softly against the beach.

For our final hike we had chosen the last 50 miles of the trail, from Lower Jo-Mary to Mount Katahdin, through an area as wild and splendid as any we had seen.

"Within these plantations of God, a decorum and sanctity reign," wrote Ralph Waldo Emerson, "a perennial festival is dressed, and the guest sees not how he should tire of them in a thousand years. In the woods, we return to reason and faith."

Maine's fall color was in its full glory, the woods ablaze with electric yellows and reds. Dead leaves already fallen to the boggy forest floor filled the air with a fragrance like that of new-mown hay. We shouldered our packs—heavy with warm clothes and food for a week—and started up the trail. Chill drops fell on our bare heads and necks as we walked beneath rain-drenched branches, and the trail was spongy with decaying needles. White birches, in clumps of three or four, shed curling strips of paper-thin bark; jays and woodpeckers flitted like shadows through the treetops.

The bogs of Maine are legendary: marshy areas where the diligence of beavers in damming streams combines with a 40-inch annual rainfall to fill low spots with clinging mud and pools of black water. The Maine

In an autumn forest near Nahmakanta Lake in Maine, volunteers Ann and Larry Clark—with daughter Rebecca peering from a backpack—cut undergrowth from the trail. They clear a 7½-mile stretch each year.

Appalachian Trail Club has put herculean effort into building walkways across most of the bogs, laying parallel logs from dry point to dry point — and off these slippery logs we took turns falling.

I was first. As I edged along a log a foot slipped, I lost my balance, jammed my walking stick into the mud, and sat down in a foot of water. My boots were wet for three days.

But I couldn't begrudge the beavers their bogs, for they have made a remarkable comeback in North America after having been nearly exterminated by three centuries of trapping. Their home was almost the entire continent until, as a 17th-century English poet wrote of adventurers in the New World:

> *. . . once 'twas Fame that led thee forth*
> *To brave the Tropick Heat, the Frozen North,*
> *Late it was Gold, then Beauty was the spur;*
> *But now our Gallants venture but for fur.*

But when fashion replaced the beaver hat with those of wool felt and silk, the trappers' markets collapsed.

The flat-tailed, amphibious rodents are fascinating creatures. Their self-sharpening front teeth, like those of all rodents, continue to grow and are kept worn down by gnawing. In the case of the beavers, the result is a prodigious tree-chopping ability: An adult beaver has been known to fell a four-inch-diameter poplar tree, cut it into sections four to eight feet long, and drag them into the water — all in one night.

Stumps gnawed to a point and mound-shaped lodges rising out of ponds are common sights in Maine. Thirty years ago a forest supervisor there reported an unusual use of the Appalachian Trail: "Mr. Bancroft . . . called at our office and reports on that part of the Trail which leaves Sterling's Pierce Pond Camps that the beavers have availed themselves of this cleared right-of-way, and that at this time they are actively engaged in yarding and skidding poplar wood for at least a quarter of a mile on an upgrade, to a small stream where they have a dam. Mr. Bancroft has some

acquaintance with the life and activities of beavers and remarked that he had never observed when beavers had carried wood up-grade before."

An 18th-century naturalist, Thomas Pennant, reported that the Indians predicted the kind of winter ahead by the size of the beavers' underwater food supply — logs and branches stored for their edible bark and twigs: "It is the Almanack of the Savages; who judge from the greater or less stock, of the mildness or severity of the approaching season."

We camped the first night at one of the Maine Forest Service campgrounds, a large clearing near a bend of Nahmakanta Stream. Crisscrossing the area were old logging roads overgrown with grass and bordered with dead branches, and with such ready fuel we soon had a roaring fire to start drying boots and trouser legs. Before bedtime I walked a hundred yards down a cleared swath to the stream to fill our canteens, my flashlight beam dancing through the tall grass ahead of me. The river was blacker than the night, but its ripples sparkled in the starlight.

As I knelt on a rock and dipped a canteen, a school of minnows spun away. From downstream came a loon's weird, demented cry. The water was icy, and I remembered that we were farther north than Montreal.

We hung our packs in an abandoned shack and spread our sleeping bags outside. The dying fire cast magic-lantern shadows against the side of the shed. About 10:30 an old, by-now-predictable sequence took place: It began to rain, and we got up and moved inside.

Breakfast was hot oatmeal, welcome in the chill dawn. The trail was another grassy logging road. We passed an abandoned truck with weeds growing up through it, looking like a relic of war on some Pacific island. Mosquitoes buzzed along in front of us; surprisingly they didn't bite, but instead flitted a couple of feet ahead as if mildly curious about us.

Fresh moose tracks the shape of huge teardrops preceded us down the trail. We were a little apprehensive about meeting one of the massive animals, for fall is the mating season when moose are temperamental and unpredictable, lumbering through the brush, knocking over small trees as

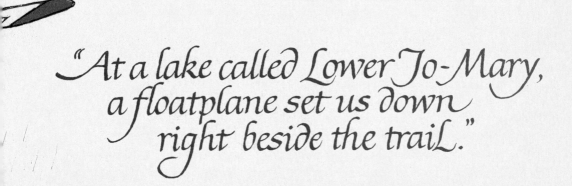

"At a lake called Lower Jo-Mary, a floatplane set us down right beside the trail."

they go. From Newfoundland come reports that the wailing horns of diesel locomotives have evoked amorous response.

We stopped for lunch on the pebbly shore of Nahmakanta Lake. The sun had come out after an overcast morning. Its warmth made us lazy, and we lingered over our coffee. That afternoon we picked our way over and through more bogs, and took off our boots and socks to cross a stream. A crow standing sentinel in a dead tree saw us coming and took off with an awkward, swooping jump to spread its raucous alarm.

At the shelter on the shore of Wadleigh Pond that night we had company: Larry and Ann Clark, their six-month-old daughter Rebecca, and their two lively German shepherd dogs, who promptly retrieved every stick thrown into the pond for them. The Clarks had taken up a brief residence in the shelter while doing volunteer maintenance work on the seven and a half miles of trail along Nahmakanta Lake. Becky, well bundled against the chill, played happily in her crib in the shelter.

In the morning we watched the Clarks tackle the job, armed with a chain saw for cutting blown-down trees, and long-handled shears for trimming weeds and brush. Becky, strapped to her mother's back, grinned with delight as Ann stooped to chop some weeds.

"My father has been in charge of maintaining this section for about ten years," Larry said, "but he couldn't come with us this time. We come in here two or three weekends a year to clear the trail, and we repaint the blazes every couple of years.

"That beaver bog you came through was just a swampy area until this year, when the beavers dammed it. I guess if the water gets much higher we'll have to relocate the trail."

The Appalachian Trail in Maine stretches 275 miles from the New Hampshire line to Mount Katahdin. When the trail idea was first being explored, the planners found the Maine wilderness so rugged they considered making Mount Washington the northern terminus instead of Katahdin. But a special study finished in 1933 reported a feasible route utilizing old logging roads and paths, and it was adopted.

In 1935 the trail construction in Maine became a project of the Civilian Conservation Corps, as it did in several other areas; and until disbandment of the corps shortly after the United States' entry into World War II, CCC crews did yeoman service. In Maine they built about 20 shelters—several are still in use—brought old trail up to standard, cleared new sections, and painted blazes. We had seen elsewhere, notably in the Blue Ridge, CCC-engineered and constructed switchbacks that have withstood the destructive forces of erosion for 35 years.

Helon Taylor, a deputy game warden in Maine for many years and later superintendent of Baxter State Park, worked with the CCC during the late 1930's, based at a camp at Flagstaff Lake. He laid out several sections of trail, including one we would later hike from Rainbow Ledges to the West Branch of the Penobscot River.

"The boys were very proud to be chosen to do this work," he told me. "Some of them were Maine boys, but they came from all over. If they were working within, say, five miles of a road, they'd take a truck back to camp at night. But beyond five miles they'd pitch their tents and camp out. Or build a lean-to and work out of it for a while. Everybody shared cooking duties and the firewood detail. Here in Maine it was mostly a matter of just clearing trail and painting blazes, but the boys loved it. We owe them a great debt."

Pollywog Stream presented us with a formidable barrier: 20 feet wide, shallow but icy cold, with a fast current. There was no way to cross except by wading. Our packs swaying precariously, our bare, numbed feet slipping on the mossy rocks, we made it safely across. On the far bank we played hide-and-seek with a pair of chipmunks whose burrow was beneath a rotting stump. Chased in the front entrance, they would immediately emerge at the back, chattering indignantly. A short distance beyond we passed the ruins of a logging camp, rusting machinery half-buried in the grass, a long handsaw leaning against a tree.

A T RAINBOW LAKE a huge boulder extended into the water like a pier, and from the end of it we got our first view of our goal: Mount Katahdin, rising cold and stolid ten air miles away. Its top third was the gray of granite, its middle zone the green of conifers, its base the rust and gold of deciduous fall foliage. Clouds passing over the mountain sent dark shadows racing down its slopes.

I sat there for a long time, gazing at it. Every mountain, they say, has a personality, but sometimes — just as with people — it takes a while to get acquainted. At this first meeting all Katahdin suggested to me was great age, permanence, and absolute indifference.

I tried to imagine the feelings of those hardy hikers who walk the trail its entire length, when they reach this spot and have the end in sight. So far about 50 have accomplished the feat in a single summer — 20 of them in 1971. But I soon came back to our own remaining challenge. We still had two days of hiking just to reach Katahdin's base.

In the shelter beside the lake that night, the mice were the most persistent yet. Once I even crawled out of my sleeping bag to try to put a stop to the sounds of gnawing and scratching that came from the packs. As I shone my flashlight into the depths of my bag, a tiny gray head with two bright, inquiring eyes turned upward, seemingly unafraid. I remembered a tale a man in southwestern Virginia had told me of a hike here in Maine the year before. He and his friends were staying overnight in a shelter with a roof of long, thin logs with shingles over them. Mice scurrying back and forth between the logs and the shingles would dangle their tails down through the cracks, and the hikers would reach up occasionally to pull a tail. Each pull produced a startled squeak.

We finally fell asleep to the intermittent quacking of ducks out on the lake. In the morning, I found the mice had kept trying. I dumped a blizzard of shredded paper from my pack, and found that my new sweatshirt had a hole in its turtle neck; but the food was untouched.

In the lean-to register a recent hiker had written: "Heading south — Caratunk probably. Most of the summer folks and foreigners have gone for the year, so now me and the critters can get ready for winter. (If we make it through hunting season.)"

It is at Caratunk that the trail crosses the swift Kennebec River.

"At the summit, at summer's end... a time for a toast."

Sometimes the water is shallow enough to be waded, but ferry service is available by arrangement. The postmaster handles inquiries.

The day was perfect for hiking—the air crisp, the sun warm, the leaves brittle underfoot. A pileated woodpecker—a large, shy black and white bird with a brilliant red crest—flapped through the treetops near a pond. On Rainbow Ledges, a naked outcropping of sun-warmed boulders, we stopped for lunch and a chat with a brother and sister hiking south toward Monson. "He's the only person who can stand to spend two weeks with me in the woods," the young woman commented.

We kept an eye on Katahdin, looming gradually closer, its summit looking peaceful and warm though it was probably biting cold.

I nearly got us lost in the afternoon. Leading the way, I missed a blaze as the trail branched off an old logging road, and we walked half a mile in a wrong direction. But if we hadn't made the mistake, we wouldn't have seen a furious grouse hen chase a squeaking chipmunk 20 yards through the dry leaves.

It was nearly dark when we crossed the highway bridge across the West Branch of the Penobscot and arrived at the deserted Abol Bridge Campground. Picnic tables were already stacked for the winter, and the river water was as cold as if it had come from a refrigerator. In fading light we rummaged for wood along the riverbank, and it was a chilled and quiet threesome that gathered around the fire.

A century before, Thoreau had camped very close to this spot during one of his trips into the Maine woods. We were within casting distance of the mouth of Abol Stream—called Aboljacknagesic in Thoreau's day—where he and his companions fished: "... the true trout ... and the silvery roaches, swallowed the bait as fast as we could throw in; and the finest specimens of both that I have ever seen, the largest one weighing three pounds...." They pitched their tent on the bank of the Penobscot, and "night shut down at last, not a little deepened by the dark side of Ktaadn, which, like a permanent shadow, reared itself from the eastern bank."

A dream awakened Thoreau in the night, so he was up before dawn.

"There stood Ktaadn with distinct and cloudless outline in the moonlight; and the rippling of the rapids was the only sound to break the stillness."

Before getting into my sleeping bag I put on every article of clothing I had with me—long fishnet underwear, trousers, two sweatshirts, a down vest, and wool socks; nevertheless, I thought I would surely freeze as the cold seeped up from the ground through every layer. In the night a fox tried to get into the packs; we heard scuffling, dragging sounds, and my flashlight beam caught a bushy, reddish-brown tail slinking off beneath a pile of picnic tables.

In the morning the sleeping bags were specked with ice. Thick mist floated over the river. Katahdin's peak was silver with frost.

Across Abol and Katahdin Streams we met a partridge hunter who had been out three days but had seen no birds. Then we began the gentle climb along the east bank of Nesowadnehunk Stream, an untamed torrent that thundered as it rushed toward the Penobscot. Where flat boulders reached into the stream, we rested in the sun as the white water swirled past. Later, when I dipped up a drink at the foot of a waterfall, the water's force nearly tore the cup from my hand. In Grassy Pond, Katahdin's reflection shimmered and then vanished as a flock of quacking ducks took off to form a ragged V overhead.

Another swamp slowed us down, and again it was almost dark when we reached Katahdin Stream Campground. The ranger in charge let us spend the night in a cabin used during the summer by a park work crew; a little wood-burning stove glowed and hissed, and soon had the cabin warm. We slept well that night, on the toe of the giant, and awoke before dawn ready for the ascent.

"By six o'clock," Thoreau had recorded, "having mounted our packs and a good blanketful of trout, ready dressed, and swung up such baggage and provision as we wished to leave behind upon the tops of saplings, to be out of reach of bears, we started for the summit of the mountain. . . ." We had no trout, but otherwise our procedure was the same.

For a mile we hiked through level forest, then began to climb. At eight c'clock we stopped for a cold breakfast; at ten we entered the clouds. They closed in tight around us, gray wisps floating past. Far down to our left, we could hear the roar of a waterfall; it gradually faded to a murmur. The trees got smaller and the boulders larger; at the Gateway we climbed with the aid of rungs hammered into the rocks.

We began to think we were on a boulder-strewn treadmill, for the mountaintop seemed constantly to recede. But at last, shortly past noon, we reached the broad plateau called the Tableland. A final short effort would take us to Katahdin's summit.

The approach looked to Thoreau "as if some time it had rained rocks, and they lay as they fell on the mountain sides. . . . They were the raw material of a planet dropped from an unseen quarry. . . ."

We stood looking at the boulders, and then at the curtain of gray cloud surrounding us. And suddenly a small miracle happened.

Through the mist the sun grew brighter, and then a spot of blue sky appeared, and another, and then a patch of green valley. With a sudden, final parting the clouds vanished, and we stood in bright sunshine with Maine at our feet. A map of green and gold forest rolled away to the horizon, with lakes and ponds scattered across it like shards of glass from a shattered window pane.

Its morning's work finished, the wind died away, and an unearthly silence enwrapped us.

Together the three of us climbed the final incline to the small signboard at the top: 5,267 feet—only a few feet less than a mile above sea level. Here the white-paint blazes ended.

We sat for a while, leaning against the sign, sharing our last chocolate bar and a sip of brandy. At the spring equinox this signboard, marking the end of the Appalachian Trail, is the first spot in the United States touched by the morning sun.

So we would close the circle: As we had begun our adventure by climbing a mountain in Georgia, we would end it by descending one in Maine. And I would find that my most vivid memories are flashes of pure color and joyous sound: the jet-black glint of a hawk's eye; an unseen songbird's trill; the gleam of gold flakes in Amy Trammell's iron pan; a blue butterfly in Vermont; a Cherokee child's sudden laugh; the sweet, red juice of wild strawberries.

Beneath an azure sky as clear as a Maine lake, we lifted our packs and started down. A little flock of snow buntings the color of clouds erupted from the rocks and scattered, like a handful of confetti.

Probing for insects, a yellow-bellied sapsucker drills into a birch tree.

"We'll always remember Maine's wild beauty."

In Maine woods strewn with maple leaves, Ron and Jill follow an abandoned dirt road cleared by logging crews. "We had a real wilderness trip through most of Maine," Jill reported. "It was the middle of October and we were alone most of the time; few people hike then because of the chance of snow. All we heard was the scuffling of our feet through the leaves." Laden with pack and sleeping bag, Ron fords frigid Pollywog Stream using his bamboo walking stick for balance. Outside a cabin left from lumbering days, he warms his feet by a campfire. "We welcomed the protection of that rough and gloomy little cabin," he said, "when it started raining in the middle of the night."

Ducks take wing from Rainbow Lake. As the morning fog lifted, Mount Katahdin

appeared across the water, giving Ron, Dick, and Jill their first glimpse of trail's end.

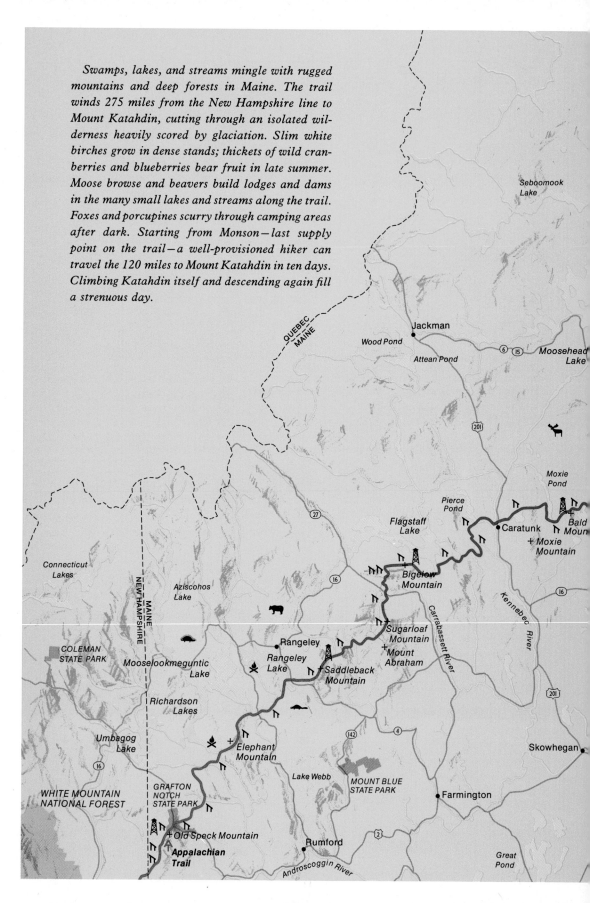

Swamps, lakes, and streams mingle with rugged mountains and deep forests in Maine. The trail winds 275 miles from the New Hampshire line to Mount Katahdin, cutting through an isolated wilderness heavily scored by glaciation. Slim white birches grow in dense stands; thickets of wild cranberries and blueberries bear fruit in late summer. Moose browse and beavers build lodges and dams in the many small lakes and streams along the trail. Foxes and porcupines scurry through camping areas after dark. Starting from Monson—last supply point on the trail—a well-provisioned hiker can travel the 120 miles to Mount Katahdin in ten days. Climbing Katahdin itself and descending again fill a strenuous day.

QUEBEC
MAINE

NEW HAMPSHIRE
MAINE

Seboomook Lake

Jackman

Wood Pond

Attean Pond

6 15

Moosehead Lake

201

Moxie Pond

Pierce Pond

Flagstaff Lake

Caratunk

Bald Moun

Moxie Mountain

Bigelow Mountain

16

Connecticut Lakes

Aziscohos Lake

Kennebec River

Carrabassett River

16

Sugarloaf Mountain

Mount Abraham

Rangeley

COLEMAN STATE PARK

Mooselookmeguntic Lake

Rangeley Lake

Saddleback Mountain

Richardson Lakes

142

4

201

Umbagog Lake

Elephant Mountain

Lake Webb

MOUNT BLUE STATE PARK

Skowhegan

16

Farmington

WHITE MOUNTAIN NATIONAL FOREST

GRAFTON NOTCH STATE PARK

Old Speck Mountain

Appalachian Trail

Rumford

2

Androscoggin River

Great Pond

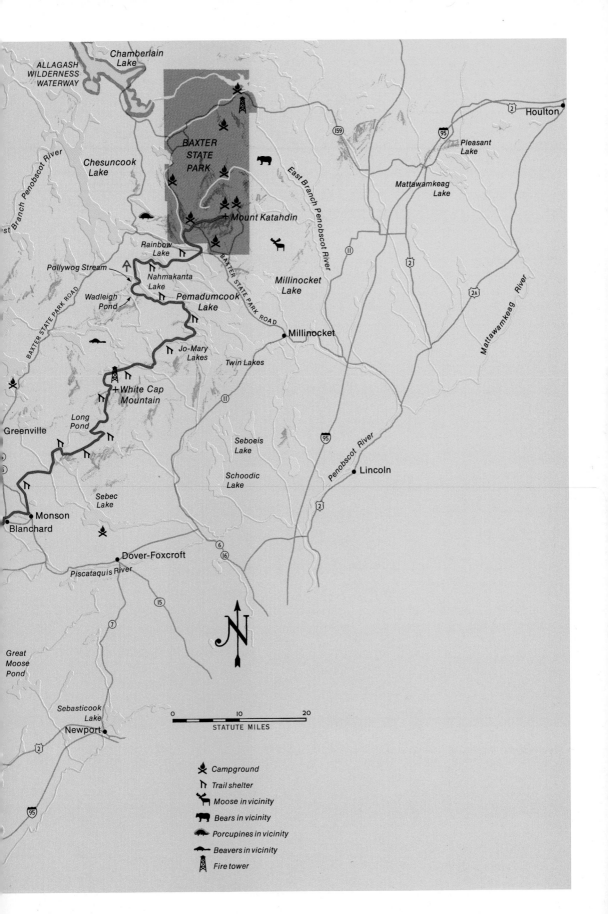

ALLAGASH
WILDERNESS
WATERWAY

Chamberlain Lake

Chesuncook Lake

BAXTER STATE PARK

st Branch Penobscot River

East Branch Penobscot River

+ Mount Katahdin

159

2 *Houlton*

95

Pleasant Lake

Mattawamkeag Lake

Rainbow Lake

BAXTER STATE PARK ROAD

Pollywog Stream

Nahmakanta Lake

Wadleigh Pond

Pemadumcook Lake

Millinocket Lake

Jo-Mary Lakes

Millinocket

11

2

2A

Mattawamkeag River

+ White Cap Mountain

Twin Lakes

11

Long Pond

Greenville

Seboeis Lake

95

Schoodic Lake

Penobscot River

Lincoln

Sebec Lake

2

Monson

Blanchard

Dover-Foxcroft

6

Piscataquis River

16

15

7

N

Great Moose Pond

Sebasticook Lake

Newport

2

0   10   20
STATUTE MILES

95

Campground

Trail shelter

Moose in vicinity

Bears in vicinity

Porcupines in vicinity

Beavers in vicinity

Fire tower

Jumble of boulders confronts the hikers as they scramble toward the summit of 5,267-foot Katahdin—their final climb. Nearing the top (left), they cross a stretch of barren rock surrounded by clouds. "...I entered within the skirts of the cloud which seemed forever drifting over the summit ..." wrote Thoreau of his 1846 ascent of the mountain. "Our hike was reminiscent of his account," Ron said. "Clouds wrapped us the entire way up; but they broke at the top, leaving us a view of what seemed to be all of Maine."

Placid stillness of Grassy Pond—near the foot of Katahdin—mirrors Doubletop Mountain and a ring of aspens and pines. Feeding on water plants at dusk, a young moose wades Sandy Stream Pond in Baxter State Park. "The night after we climbed Katahdin—our final night on the trail—we camped near Grassy Pond and sat up late by the fire reflecting on our trip," Ron recalled. "We had spent three seasons hiking a slice of America. I lost 15 pounds, and grew a full, bushy beard. I made new friends from Georgia to Maine, yet discovered an affinity for solitude. And I found a refuge for my city-battered spirit in the quiet woods and heights of the Appalachians."

Before you hike...
AN EPILOGUE

"HE WHO is indeed of the brotherhood," wrote Robert Louis Stevenson of walkers, "does not voyage in quest of the picturesque, but of certain jolly humours—of the hope and spirit with which the march begins at morning, and the peace and spiritual repletion of the evening's rest. He cannot tell whether he puts his knapsack on, or takes it off, with more delight.

"The excitement of the departure puts him in key for that of the arrival. Whatever he does is not only a reward in itself, but will be further rewarded in the sequel; and so pleasure leads on to pleasure in an endless chain."

But the endless chain can be less than pleasurable if a hiker sets out unprepared.

If you are planning a hike on the Appalachian Trail, I suggest you start by sending 25 cents to the Appalachian Trail Conference, Box 236, Harpers Ferry, West Virginia 25425. The conference staff will send you information that includes a brief history of the trail, a summary of its route, a list of pertinent publications, and an application for conference membership. If you join you will pay annual dues of seven dollars and receive a quarterly bulletin, *Appalachian Trailway News.*

The conference and its affiliated clubs publish ten guidebooks and several pamphlets. *Lightweight Equipment for Hiking, Camping, and Mountaineering* describes recommended equipment and provides names and addresses of suppliers; *Suggestions for Appalachian Trail Users* lists guidebooks and maps, and includes essays on trail etiquette, precautions, shelters, equipment, clothing, and food. Each of the official guidebooks covers a section of the trail, providing a detailed description of the route, specifying locations of water sources and shelters, identifying intersecting highways, listing nearby accommodations, and setting forth state fire regulations.

Most of the guidebooks include route maps; all of them indicate map sources. Applicable U. S. Geological Survey and Tennessee Valley Authority quadrangles are listed; they are available from the USGS Division of Distribution, 1200 S. Eads Street, Arlington, Va. 22202. U. S. Forest Service maps are supplied by the Regional Forester, 633 W. Wisconsin Ave., Milwaukee, Wis. 53203, for national forests in New England; and by the Regional Forester, 1720 Peachtree Road N.W., Atlanta, Ga. 30309, for those farther south.

The two things that usually cause the most grief for a novice hiker are his feet. Devote the time, trouble, and money necessary to acquire a good pair of hiking boots. Sneakers and other light sports shoes won't do, except for a short, casual walk. On extended hikes they not only are bad for your feet but also wear out quickly. Break in your boots with short periods of wear before starting a serious hike. Carry plenty of adhesive bandages—you're bound to have some blisters—and a small bottle of antiseptic. Take along a first-aid manual.

Most novice hikers try to carry too much weight. As you assemble your pack, eliminate ruthlessly. Remember that ounces quickly add up to pounds. Some experienced hikers go so far as to trim the borders from maps and discard candy bar wrappers before starting out. As you struggle up a steep ridge you'll be glad you left your old Boy Scout hatchet at home.

Preliminary conditioning pays off. Starting gradually, take up regular jogging or jumping rope several weeks before leaving.

It's wise to carry a lightweight backpacking stove. Firewood is often unavailable or difficult to find in heavily traveled sections. If you find plenty, use some for a small, cheery fire in the evening, but do your cooking on a stove.

The final words of advice I leave to John Kieran, who wrote on walking in 1953: "Take to the woods on windy days. It's quieter there. Keep your ears open. You can always hear more birds than you can see. Keep your eyes open. There are flowers in bloom through most months of the year, and trees are as interesting even in early spring as they are in summer.... Take the sun over your shoulder for the best views. Avoid slippery footing as you would the plague, and don't sit on damp ground. Keep walking."

Acknowledgments

The Special Publications Division is grateful to the people named or quoted in this
book and to those listed here for their generous cooperation and assistance: Stanley
A. Murray, Chairman, and Lester L. Holmes, Executive Director, Appalachian Trail
Conference; Walter A. Anderson, Glenn L. Bowers, Joan R. Gibson, Alfred K. Guthe,
Richard W. Iobst, Roxie C. Laybourne, Robert B. Neuman, Keith R. Shea, Stanwyn
G. Shetler, Arthur A. Socolow, and Richard L. Zusi; the National Park Service, the
U. S. Forest Service, and the Vermont Historical Society.

Additional Reading

Maurice Brooks, *The Appalachians;* F. Allen Burt, *The Story of Mount Washington;*
John C. Campbell, *The Southern Highlander and His Homeland;* John A. Caruso, *The
Appalachian Frontier;* Thomas L. Connelly, *Discovering the Appalachians;* Colin
Fletcher, *The Complete Walker;* Michael Frome, *Whose Woods These Are: The Story
of the National Forests;* Edward B. Garvey, *Appalachian Hiker;* Euell Gibbons, *Stalk-
ing the Wild Asparagus;* Horace Kephart, *Our Southern Highlanders;* Roderick Peattie,
The Great Smokies and the Blue Ridge; Eliot Porter, *Appalachian Wilderness: The
Great Smoky Mountains;* Aaron Sussman and Ruth Goode, *The Magic of Walking;* Ann
and Myron Sutton, *The Appalachian Trail.* In NATIONAL GEOGRAPHIC: Andrew H.
Brown, "Skyline Trail from Maine to Georgia," August 1949; William O. Douglas,
"The Friendly Huts of the White Mountains," August 1961; and Val Hart, "Pack Trip
Through the Smokies," October 1952. Readers may also wish to consult the National
Geographic Index for related material.

Composition for *The Appalachian Trail* by National Geographic's Phototypographic
Division, John E. McConnell, Manager. Posterization and tone-lines photomechani-
cally prepared in the National Geographic Photographic Laboratories, Carl M. Shrader,
Chief. Printed and bound by Fawcett Printing Corp., Rockville, Md. Color separations
by Graphic Color Plate, Inc., Stamford, Conn.; The Lanman Company, Alexandria,
Va.; Lebanon Valley Offset Company, Inc., Annville, Pa.; and Progressive Color Corp.,
Rockville, Md.